Lyra Thorne

Defying Gender Oppression in Kyriden – Unauthorized

Kiran Kwon

ISBN: 9781779697844
Imprint: Telephasic Workshop
Copyright © 2024 Kiran Kwon.
All Rights Reserved.

Contents

Introduction: Who the Fuck Is Lyra Thorne?

The Fucking Rebel Leader of Kyriden: How Lyra Thorne Led the Fight Against Gender Oppression

Breaking the Fucking Chains: How Lyra Rose from the Fucking Margins to Become a Fucking Revolutionary Icon

Lyra Thorne didn't just wake up one day and decide to become a fucking revolutionary icon. No, her journey was forged in the fires of oppression, where she learned the hard truths about the systemic fucking barriers that kept her and her people shackled to the margins of Kyriden society. This section dives deep into the gritty reality of her rise, highlighting the struggles, strategies, and sheer fucking tenacity that propelled her from the fringes to the forefront of the gender rights revolution.

The Margins of Kyriden: A Landscape of Oppression

In Kyriden, gender oppression wasn't just a concept; it was a daily fucking reality. The societal structure was built on a foundation of patriarchal norms that dictated the roles and rights of women and gender minorities. The prevailing theory of gender roles, as articulated by Judith Butler in her seminal work *Gender Trouble*, posits that gender is performative—meaning it's a set of behaviors and roles enforced by societal expectations. In Kyriden, this performance was rigidly scripted, leaving little room for deviation.

Lyra's early life was a testament to this oppressive framework. Born into a family that adhered strictly to traditional gender roles, she faced relentless pressure to conform. The systemic barriers were reinforced by cultural narratives that

1

marginalized her identity. As she later recounted in her speeches, "I was told who I was supposed to be, but I knew in my fucking bones that I was meant for more."

The Awakening: Realizing the Need for Change

The turning point in Lyra's life came when she witnessed the brutal treatment of a close friend who dared to defy gender norms. This event ignited a fire within her—a realization that the chains of oppression could only be broken through collective action. Inspired by the works of bell hooks and her emphasis on intersectionality, Lyra began to see the interconnectedness of struggles faced by various marginalized groups.

This awakening was not without its challenges. Lyra faced backlash from her community, ostracized for her radical thoughts and actions. Yet, she persisted, drawing strength from the underground movements that had begun to emerge in Kyriden. These groups, often operating in secrecy, were crucial in shaping her understanding of activism. They taught her the importance of solidarity and the need for a multifaceted approach to fighting oppression.

Building the Movement: Strategies and Solidarity

As Lyra began organizing protests and meetings, she quickly learned that effective leadership required more than just passion; it demanded strategy. Utilizing the principles of nonviolent resistance articulated by figures like Martin Luther King Jr., she crafted a plan that would resonate with the people of Kyriden. Her approach was rooted in the belief that "the power of the people is greater than the people in power."

One of her first major actions was the *March for Equality*, which brought together a diverse coalition of women, LGBTQ+ individuals, and allies. The event was a fucking spectacle, drawing thousands to the streets of Kyriden's capital. Lyra's speeches, infused with raw emotion and sharp critique, rallied the crowd. She famously declared, "We are not just fighting for our rights; we are fighting for our fucking lives!" This pivotal moment marked the beginning of her ascent as a revolutionary icon.

The Government's Response: Brutal Repression

However, with rising visibility came increased scrutiny and repression from the Kyriden government. Lyra faced threats, harassment, and even arrests, yet she remained undeterred. The government's attempts to silence her only fueled her resolve. As she noted in her memoirs, "Every time they tried to break me, I found new strength in the voices of those who stood beside me."

The brutal tactics employed by the state were a stark reminder of the risks involved in activism. Yet, Lyra understood that fear was a weapon wielded by oppressors, and she refused to let it dictate her actions. Instead, she transformed her experiences of persecution into rallying cries for justice, emphasizing the need for resilience in the face of adversity.

Legacy of Resistance: The Making of a Revolutionary Icon

Through her relentless efforts, Lyra Thorne emerged not just as a leader but as a fucking symbol of resistance. She became the face of the movement, a beacon of hope for those still trapped in the margins. Her story resonated beyond Kyriden, inspiring activists across the galaxy to rise against their own forms of oppression.

In the words of famed activist Audre Lorde, "Your silence will not protect you." Lyra's journey from the margins to the forefront exemplified this truth. She broke the fucking chains of oppression, not just for herself but for countless others. Her legacy serves as a powerful reminder that change is possible when individuals dare to defy the status quo and fight for their rights.

In conclusion, the rise of Lyra Thorne from the margins to become a revolutionary icon was not merely an individual triumph; it was a collective awakening. Her story embodies the struggle against systemic oppression and the enduring power of solidarity. As Kyriden continues to grapple with its legacy of gender inequality, Lyra's fight remains a vital chapter in the ongoing narrative of resistance and liberation.

The Fucking Oppression of Women and Gender Minorities on Kyriden: Why Thorne's Leadership Was Fucking Necessary

On the planet Kyriden, the systemic oppression of women and gender minorities is not just a social issue; it's a fucking institution. The societal norms that govern Kyriden are steeped in patriarchal traditions that dictate every aspect of life, from the roles individuals are expected to play to the rights they are afforded. In this context, Lyra Thorne emerged as a beacon of hope, challenging a status quo that had long marginalized and silenced voices that deserved to be heard.

Theoretical Framework of Gender Oppression

To understand the necessity of Thorne's leadership, one must first grasp the theoretical underpinnings of gender oppression on Kyriden. Drawing on feminist theory, particularly the works of scholars like Judith Butler and bell hooks, we can analyze how gender is not merely a binary construct but a spectrum that has been historically misrepresented and oppressed.   Butler's theory of performativity suggests that gender is a socially constructed identity, reinforced by repeated behaviors and societal expectations. This is evident in Kyriden's rigid gender roles, which dictate that women and gender minorities must conform to specific behaviors and appearances, often at the cost of their autonomy and identity.

The concept of intersectionality, coined by Kimberlé Crenshaw, further complicates the landscape of oppression on Kyriden.   Women and gender minorities do not experience oppression in isolation; rather, their experiences are shaped by intersecting identities, including race, class, and sexual orientation. For instance, a queer woman of color in Kyriden faces unique challenges that are distinct from those experienced by her white, heterosexual counterparts. This intersectional lens is crucial in understanding why Thorne's leadership was not only necessary but urgent.

The Reality of Gender Oppression on Kyriden

The fucking reality on Kyriden is grim. Women are often relegated to the domestic sphere, expected to fulfill roles as caretakers and homemakers while being denied access to education and employment opportunities. Gender minorities face even harsher realities, with many subjected to violence, discrimination, and systemic exclusion from societal participation. Reports indicate that over 70% of women in Kyriden have experienced some form of gender-based violence, while gender minorities are disproportionately affected by hate crimes and state-sanctioned violence.

One prominent example of this oppression is the enforcement of the "Traditional Values Act," a draconian law that criminalizes non-conformity to gender norms. Under this act, individuals who do not adhere to prescribed gender roles face severe penalties, including imprisonment and public shaming. This law serves as a tool of control, perpetuating the cycle of fear and oppression that Thorne sought to dismantle.

The Necessity of Thorne's Leadership

In this oppressive climate, Thorne's leadership became a fucking necessity. Her rise as a revolutionary leader was not merely a response to the injustices faced by women and gender minorities; it was a clarion call for systemic change. Thorne recognized that the fight for gender equality could not be won in isolation. It required a united front, a coalition of marginalized voices ready to challenge the fucking status quo.

Thorne's strategic approach involved mobilizing grassroots movements, educating the public about their rights, and creating safe spaces for dialogue and activism. She understood that the power of resistance lay in collective action, and she worked tirelessly to build alliances with other marginalized groups, including the LGBTQ+ community, racial minorities, and working-class activists. This intersectional approach not only broadened the base of support for the gender rights movement but also enriched the discourse surrounding oppression on Kyriden.

In her speeches, Thorne often invoked the idea of "fucking solidarity," emphasizing that the fight for gender rights is intrinsically linked to the struggles of all oppressed peoples. Her ability to articulate these connections made her a fucking revolutionary icon, inspiring countless individuals to join the movement and stand up against the systemic forces that sought to silence them.

Conclusion: The Legacy of Thorne's Leadership

Thorne's leadership was not just about challenging oppressive laws; it was about redefining the narrative surrounding gender on Kyriden. By elevating the voices of women and gender minorities, she illuminated the pervasive injustices that had long been ignored. Her work laid the foundation for a movement that sought not only to dismantle oppressive structures but also to foster a culture of inclusivity and respect for all identities.

As Kyriden stands on the precipice of change, the legacy of Lyra Thorne serves as a powerful reminder that leadership in the fight against oppression is not just necessary; it is fucking transformative. Her journey from the margins to the forefront of the gender rights revolution exemplifies the potential for change when individuals refuse to accept the status quo and instead choose to fight for a future where everyone, regardless of gender identity, can live freely and authentically.

In the end, Thorne's leadership was fucking necessary because it illuminated a path forward in a society that had long been shrouded in darkness. The fight for gender equality on Kyriden is far from over, but with Thorne's indomitable spirit guiding the way, the future looks fucking bright.

How Thorne Built the Fucking Movement for Gender Equality on a Planet Steeped in Fucking Tradition

On the planet Kyriden, where tradition is as thick as the smog that blankets its cities, Lyra Thorne emerged as a beacon of hope for those shackled by the oppressive weight of gender norms. In a society that revered patriarchal structures, the fight for gender equality was not just a battle; it was a fucking revolution. Thorne's approach to building this movement was both strategic and deeply personal, drawing upon her own experiences of oppression and the collective pain of marginalized communities.

The Fucking Foundation: Understanding Tradition and Oppression

Kyriden's societal framework was built upon centuries of rigid gender roles, where women and gender minorities were relegated to the sidelines of existence. The concept of gender was not just a social construct; it was a fucking prison. The traditionalists wielded their customs like weapons, enforcing norms that dictated everything from clothing to career choices. Thorne recognized that to dismantle this oppressive system, one must first understand its roots.

$$\text{Oppression}_{\text{Kyriden}} = f(\text{Tradition, Patriarchy, Culture}) \qquad (1)$$

This equation illustrates that the oppression faced by individuals on Kyriden is a function of intertwined elements of tradition, patriarchy, and culture. Thorne's strategy involved dissecting these elements to expose their fragility. By doing so, she aimed to create a narrative that resonated with the oppressed and challenged the status quo.

Building Alliances: The Power of Collective Action

Thorne understood that individual struggles were interconnected. She began to forge alliances with other marginalized groups, recognizing that the fight for gender equality was part of a broader struggle against systemic oppression. This coalition-building was pivotal; it transformed the movement from a solitary fight into a collective uprising.

$$\text{Movement Strength} = \sum_{i=1}^{n} \text{Alliances}_i \qquad (2)$$

Here, Movement Strength is directly proportional to the number of alliances formed. Thorne's ability to unite disparate groups—such as LGBTQ+

communities, racial minorities, and labor activists—created a powerful force that could not be ignored. Each protest, each rally, became a testament to the strength found in unity.

Harnessing the Fucking Power of Education

Education became one of Thorne's most potent tools in dismantling the oppressive structures of Kyriden. She launched underground workshops that educated people about their rights, the history of gender oppression, and the importance of activism. These sessions were not merely informational; they were transformative, igniting a fire in the hearts of those who attended.

$$Awareness = Education \times Engagement \tag{3}$$

In this equation, Awareness increases as a product of Education and Engagement. Thorne's workshops encouraged active participation, turning passive listeners into active participants in the fight for equality.

Strategic Protests: The Art of Visibility

Visibility was crucial in Thorne's movement. She organized protests that not only drew attention to gender issues but also highlighted the absurdity of Kyriden's traditions. These demonstrations were carefully planned, often taking place during significant cultural events, thereby ensuring maximum exposure.

For example, during the Festival of Tradition—a celebration of Kyriden's historical customs—Thorne led a counter-protest that showcased the voices of those marginalized by these very traditions. Signs reading "Tradition Doesn't Equal Oppression" and "Our Gender, Our Choice" flooded the streets, challenging the narrative that tradition was synonymous with morality.

$$Impact = Visibility \times Media\ Coverage \tag{4}$$

This equation posits that the Impact of a protest is a function of its Visibility and the Media Coverage it receives. Thorne's strategic use of social media amplified the reach of these protests, allowing the message to transcend Kyriden's borders.

Creating a Fucking Cultural Shift

Thorne's movement was not just about immediate change; it aimed to create a cultural shift. By employing art, music, and literature, she infused the movement with a sense of identity and purpose. Artists and musicians were encouraged to express their struggles through their work, creating a rich tapestry of resistance that resonated with the populace.

$$Cultural\ Shift = Art + Activism \tag{5}$$

In this equation, a Cultural Shift occurs when Art and Activism converge. Thorne's ability to integrate these elements not only galvanized her supporters but also attracted those who may have been indifferent to the cause.

Conclusion: The Fucking Road Ahead

Lyra Thorne's journey in building the movement for gender equality on Kyriden was fraught with challenges, yet it was marked by resilience and creativity. By understanding the deep-rooted traditions that upheld oppression, forging alliances, harnessing education, staging impactful protests, and fostering a cultural shift, Thorne laid the groundwork for a revolution that would echo through the ages.

As the movement continues to evolve, the question remains: will Thorne's legacy inspire future generations to challenge the traditions that bind them? The answer lies in the hearts of those who dare to dream of a fucking equitable future. In Kyriden, the fight for gender equality is not just a battle; it is a fucking movement that refuses to be silenced.

The Fucking Power of Resistance: How Thorne United Women and Gender Minorities to Defy the Fucking System

In the heart of Kyriden, where the air was thick with the weight of tradition and oppression, Lyra Thorne emerged as a beacon of hope and defiance. The fucking power of resistance that she cultivated was not just a spontaneous eruption of anger; it was a carefully orchestrated movement that united women and gender minorities against the fucking system that sought to silence them. This section delves into the strategies, theories, and real-world examples that illustrate how Thorne's leadership galvanized a diverse coalition of marginalized voices.

Theoretical Framework: Intersectionality in Action

At the core of Thorne's revolutionary ethos was the concept of intersectionality, a term coined by Kimberlé Crenshaw. This theory posits that individuals experience oppression in overlapping and interdependent ways, particularly those at the intersection of multiple marginalized identities. Thorne understood that to challenge the fucking system effectively, she had to address the unique struggles faced by women, non-binary individuals, and gender nonconforming people in Kyriden.

$$O = f(G, R, E) \tag{6}$$

Where:

+ O = Oppression

+ G = Gender identity

+ R = Race and ethnicity

+ E = Economic status

This equation illustrates that oppression is a function of various intersecting identities, which Thorne utilized to rally her supporters. She emphasized that the fight for gender equality could not be separated from the struggles against racial, economic, and social injustices.

Building Solidarity Among Diverse Groups

Thorne's ability to unite disparate groups was rooted in her recognition of shared experiences and common goals. She organized community meetings, workshops, and rallies that brought together women from different backgrounds, queer individuals, and allies. These gatherings served as safe spaces for dialogue, allowing participants to share their stories and grievances.

One notable example was the "Fucking Unity March," which took place in the capital city of Kyriden. Thorne encouraged women and gender minorities to wear colors representing their identities—blue for trans rights, pink for women's rights, and rainbow flags for LGBTQ+ solidarity. This visual manifestation of unity was powerful, as it demonstrated that despite their differences, they were all fighting against the same oppressive system.

The Role of Art and Expression

Art became a crucial tool in Thorne's arsenal for resistance. She understood that storytelling and creative expression could evoke empathy and inspire action. Thorne initiated the "Voices of Kyriden" project, which featured poetry readings, visual art displays, and performances that highlighted the struggles of marginalized communities.

$$E = A + C \tag{7}$$

Where:

- E = Empowerment

- A = Artistic expression

- C = Community engagement

Through this equation, Thorne illustrated how artistic expression coupled with community engagement could lead to empowerment. The project not only raised awareness but also fostered a sense of belonging among participants, reinforcing the idea that they were part of a larger movement.

Strategic Alliances and Coalitions

Thorne's strategic brilliance lay in her ability to forge alliances with other marginalized groups, creating a robust coalition that could effectively challenge the status quo.   She reached out to labor unions, environmental activists, and anti-racism organizations, emphasizing the interconnectedness of their struggles.

An example of this coalition-building was the "Kyriden Alliance for Justice," which brought together diverse groups to advocate for comprehensive reforms. The alliance organized protests against the government's oppressive policies, showcasing a united front that made it difficult for authorities to dismiss their demands.

$$C_{total} = C_1 + C_2 + C_3 \tag{8}$$

Where:

- C_{total} = Total coalition strength

- C_1 = Women's rights groups

- C_2 = LGBTQ+ organizations

- C_3 = Labor unions and other marginalized groups

This equation highlights how the total strength of the coalition was a sum of its parts, demonstrating the effectiveness of solidarity in amplifying their collective voice.

The Impact of Grassroots Mobilization

Thorne's grassroots mobilization efforts were pivotal in creating a culture of resistance. She trained activists in nonviolent protest techniques and civil disobedience, empowering them to take action in their communities. The "Fuck the System" campaign, which encouraged individuals to disrupt oppressive events and practices, became a hallmark of Thorne's strategy.

One significant event was the "Night of Resistance," where activists occupied government buildings to demand policy changes. This act of defiance garnered national attention, forcing the government to acknowledge the growing discontent among the populace.

Conclusion: The Fucking Legacy of Resistance

Thorne's ability to unite women and gender minorities in Kyriden was a testament to the fucking power of resistance. By leveraging intersectionality, fostering solidarity, utilizing art, forming strategic alliances, and mobilizing grassroots efforts, she created a movement that challenged the fucking system at its core. As Thorne's legacy continues to inspire new generations of activists, her story serves as a reminder that collective action can dismantle the structures of oppression and pave the way for a more equitable future for all marginalized communities.

The Future of Kyriden: Will Thorne's Fucking Legacy Lead to Systemic Fucking Change?

Lyra Thorne's journey from the fucking margins to the forefront of the gender rights revolution on Kyriden is a testament to the power of resistance and the potential for systemic fucking change. As we look to the future of Kyriden, we must ask ourselves: will Thorne's fucking legacy pave the way for lasting transformation, or will it be another fleeting moment in the ongoing struggle for equality?

To understand the potential for systemic fucking change in Kyriden, we must first analyze the socio-political landscape that Thorne helped to shape. The fucking oppression of women and gender minorities has deep roots in Kyriden's cultural and institutional frameworks. Traditional gender roles, reinforced by a patriarchal society, have created an environment where discrimination and violence against marginalized groups are normalized. Thorne's activism, however, has sparked a fucking dialogue that challenges these entrenched beliefs.

$$\text{Systemic Change} = \text{Awareness} + \text{Mobilization} + \text{Policy Reform} \quad (9)$$

This equation illustrates that systemic fucking change is not an isolated event; it requires a combination of awareness, mobilization, and policy reform. Thorne's fucking legacy has undeniably raised awareness about gender oppression on Kyriden. Her ability to articulate the struggles of women and gender minorities has resonated with the populace, creating a collective consciousness that demands change.

Moreover, Thorne's leadership has mobilized diverse groups within Kyriden, fostering coalitions that transcend traditional boundaries. By uniting women, LGBTQ+ individuals, and other marginalized communities, she has demonstrated that the fight for equality is not just a singular battle but a fucking collective struggle. The strategic partnerships she forged with other social justice movements have amplified the impact of her message, creating a fucking ripple effect that challenges the status quo.

However, the path to systemic fucking change is fraught with challenges. The Kyriden government's historical response to Thorne's activism has been one of brutal repression. The fucking crackdown on dissenting voices poses a significant barrier to lasting change. As Thorne herself faced imprisonment and violence, it becomes evident that the fight for gender equality comes at a personal cost.

$$\text{Resistance} = \text{Courage} \times \text{Solidarity} \qquad (10)$$

This equation emphasizes that resistance is a product of both individual courage and collective solidarity. Thorne's fucking courage in the face of adversity has inspired countless others to join the fight, but sustaining this momentum will require ongoing solidarity among activists. The future of Kyriden hinges on the ability of these movements to remain united, even in the face of government oppression.

Furthermore, the role of technology in Thorne's movement cannot be underestimated. The digital age has provided activists with unprecedented tools for organizing and spreading their message. Social media platforms, encrypted communication channels, and online advocacy campaigns have enabled Thorne's legacy to reach beyond Kyriden's borders. This global connectivity offers a unique opportunity for systemic fucking change, as international attention can pressure the Kyriden government to address human rights abuses.

$$\text{Global Pressure} = \text{Media Attention} + \text{International Advocacy} \qquad (11)$$

In this equation, global pressure is derived from both media attention and international advocacy efforts. Thorne's movement has garnered significant media coverage, drawing the eyes of the galaxy to the plight of gender minorities in

Kyriden. This attention, coupled with advocacy from global organizations, creates a formidable force that can hold the Kyriden government accountable.

As we consider the future of Kyriden, it is essential to recognize that Thorne's legacy is not merely about her personal achievements but about the fucking movement she catalyzed. The question of whether her legacy will lead to systemic fucking change depends on the continued engagement of the community, the resilience of activists, and the willingness of allies to stand in solidarity.

In conclusion, the future of Kyriden is uncertain, but Thorne's fucking legacy serves as a beacon of hope. The potential for systemic fucking change exists, rooted in the awareness she has raised, the coalitions she has built, and the global attention she has attracted. If the fight for gender equality continues to evolve, adapting to new challenges and embracing innovative strategies, there is a fucking possibility that Kyriden can emerge as a leader in the struggle for gender rights. The question remains: will the people of Kyriden rise to the occasion, or will Thorne's legacy become just another chapter in the long history of oppression? Only time will tell, but one thing is for sure: the fight is far from over, and the spirit of Lyra Thorne will continue to inspire those who dare to challenge the fucking system.

The Fucking Early Years: Thorne's Path to Activism

Surviving in a Repressive Fucking Society: Thorne's Fucking Early Experiences of Gender Oppression

The Fucking Reality of Gender Roles and Fucking Oppression on Kyriden: A Society Rigged Against Women

In the vibrant yet tumultuous world of Kyriden, the landscape of gender roles is a fucking battleground. From the moment a child is born, the societal framework is designed to enforce rigid expectations based on their assigned gender. The fucking patriarchy is not merely an abstract concept here; it is a fucking reality that dictates every aspect of life, from the cradle to the grave.

The Fucking Framework of Gender Roles

In Kyriden, gender roles are deeply entrenched in cultural narratives and institutional structures. The fucking expectations placed on women and gender minorities are not only oppressive but also systematically enforced through various societal mechanisms. For instance, the concept of *masculine superiority* is prevalent, where men are regarded as the primary decision-makers in both the public and private spheres. This manifests in the workplace, where women are often relegated to subordinate roles, receiving lower wages and fewer opportunities for advancement.

Let P represent the power dynamics in Kyriden, where:

$$P = \frac{W_m}{W_f} \quad (1)$$

15

Here, W_m is the wage earned by men, and W_f is the wage earned by women. In Kyriden, this ratio often skews heavily in favor of men, illustrating the systemic economic oppression of women. The average wage gap in Kyriden is approximately 30%, with women earning only 70% of what their male counterparts make for the same fucking work.

Cultural Narratives and Socialization

The oppression of women in Kyriden is further perpetuated by cultural narratives that glorify traditional gender roles. From a young age, children are socialized into their respective roles through family dynamics, educational systems, and media portrayals. The fucking narrative that women should prioritize family over career is omnipresent, leading to the internalization of guilt and inadequacy among women who aspire to break free from these constraints.

Moreover, the concept of *gender performativity*, as theorized by Judith Butler, is highly relevant in Kyriden. Butler argues that gender is not an inherent identity but rather a series of acts and performances that are socially constructed. In Kyriden, women are expected to perform femininity—characterized by submissiveness, nurturing behavior, and emotional labor—while any deviation from this norm is met with harsh societal backlash.

Institutional Barriers to Equality

The institutional barriers to gender equality in Kyriden are staggering. Laws and policies that ostensibly promote gender equality often lack enforcement mechanisms, rendering them ineffective. For example, although there are laws against gender-based violence, the judicial system is riddled with corruption and bias, leading to a culture of impunity for perpetrators. The fucking statistics are alarming: over 60% of gender-based violence cases go unreported, and among those that are reported, less than 10% result in convictions.

Let V represent the rate of violence against women, and R the rate of reported cases:

$$V = \frac{C}{R} \quad (2)$$

Where C is the number of cases resulting in conviction. In Kyriden, this ratio indicates a fucking failure of the legal system to protect women, as many victims fear retaliation or further victimization through the legal process.

Economic Disparities and Dependency

Economic dependency is another critical aspect of gender oppression in Kyriden. Women are often confined to low-paying jobs, primarily in the service and domestic sectors, which lack benefits and job security. This economic vulnerability makes it exceedingly difficult for women to leave abusive relationships or advocate for their rights. The fucking economic model in Kyriden is designed to keep women dependent on male counterparts, reinforcing the cycle of oppression.

The economic theory of *dependency theory* posits that the economic structure of a society can perpetuate inequality. In Kyriden, the dependency of women on men for financial stability is a direct outcome of systemic discrimination in education and employment opportunities.

Conclusion: A Society Rigged Against Women

In conclusion, the reality of gender roles and oppression in Kyriden is a multifaceted issue, deeply rooted in cultural, institutional, and economic structures. The fucking system is rigged against women and gender minorities, creating a vicious cycle of oppression that is difficult to escape. Activists like Lyra Thorne recognize these challenges and strive to dismantle the fucking barriers that uphold this unjust society. The fight for gender equality in Kyriden is not just a struggle for rights; it is a battle for the very fucking soul of the planet, demanding a radical rethinking of how gender is perceived and lived.

As Kyriden stands on the brink of revolution, the question remains: will the future embrace a new paradigm of equality, or will the chains of oppression continue to bind its people?

How Thorne's Fucking Personal Struggles Led Her to Fucking Fight Back

Lyra Thorne's journey from a marginalized individual in Kyriden to a revolutionary leader was not just a product of external circumstances; it was deeply rooted in her personal struggles. These struggles served as the catalyst that ignited her passion for activism and fueled her relentless fight against gender oppression.

The Fucking Reality of Gender Oppression

In Kyriden, gender roles were not merely societal expectations; they were enforced through a complex web of cultural norms and institutionalized discrimination. Women and gender minorities faced systemic barriers that limited their opportunities, autonomy, and rights. This oppressive environment created a sense of urgency within Thorne, compelling her to confront the injustices she witnessed daily. Her early experiences were characterized by a profound sense of frustration and helplessness, as she navigated a world that constantly devalued her existence.

Personal Struggles as a Catalyst for Activism

Thorne's personal struggles were multifaceted. Growing up in a conservative household, she experienced firsthand the suffocating grip of traditional gender expectations. These experiences manifested in various forms: bullying at school, familial rejection, and a pervasive sense of isolation. Each incident chipped away at her self-esteem, but rather than succumbing to despair, Thorne channeled her pain into a fierce determination to fight back.

The turning point came when Thorne faced a particularly brutal act of discrimination that left her feeling powerless. It was during this period of intense emotional turmoil that she discovered the power of collective action. She began attending underground meetings of like-minded individuals who shared her frustrations. The camaraderie she found in these spaces was transformative; it provided her not only with a sense of belonging but also with the tools to challenge the oppressive structures around her.

The Role of Underground Movements

The underground movements in Kyriden played a crucial role in shaping Thorne's activism. These groups, often operating in secrecy due to the repressive regime, fostered a culture of resistance and resilience. Thorne learned about the history of previous uprisings, the strategies employed by past activists, and the importance of solidarity among marginalized communities. This education was pivotal in her development as a leader; she realized that her personal struggles were not isolated incidents but part of a larger narrative of oppression that required a collective response.

Early Fucking Protests: The Birth of a Leader

Thorne's first foray into activism was marked by her participation in early protests organized by these underground movements. These demonstrations were often small and risky, yet they were infused with a palpable energy that inspired Thorne. She began to understand the significance of visibility and representation; her presence at these events was a declaration of her identity and a rejection of the oppressive norms that sought to silence her.

During one particularly impactful protest, Thorne witnessed the brutality of the government's response to dissent. This experience solidified her resolve to fight back. The sight of fellow activists being arrested and beaten ignited a fire within her—a realization that the stakes were higher than she had ever imagined. It was no longer just about her personal struggles; it was about the future of countless individuals who faced similar oppression.

The Fucking Emotional Toll of Activism

However, the path of activism was not without its challenges. Thorne faced significant emotional and mental tolls as she navigated the complexities of leading a movement while grappling with her own trauma. The weight of responsibility was heavy; she often questioned whether she was doing enough to honor the sacrifices of those who came before her. The fear of failure loomed large, but it was counterbalanced by the hope that her efforts could lead to meaningful change.

The Future of Fucking Gender Resistance Movements

Thorne's personal struggles were not just a backdrop to her activism; they were integral to her identity as a leader. She emerged from her battles with a profound understanding of the need for intersectionality in the fight for gender rights. Her experiences taught her that the fight against gender oppression could not be separated from the struggles of other marginalized groups. This insight would later inform her strategies for building coalitions and fostering solidarity within the broader movement.

As Thorne reflected on her journey, she recognized that her personal struggles had equipped her with the empathy and resilience necessary to lead a revolution. Her story became a beacon of hope for others facing similar challenges, inspiring a new generation of activists to rise up and fight back against the oppressive forces that sought to silence them. The future of gender resistance movements depended on individuals like Thorne—those who were willing to confront their own demons and transform their pain into a powerful force for change.

The Fucking Role of Underground Movements in Shaping Thorne's Fucking Activism

In the oppressive landscape of Kyriden, where traditional norms were deeply entrenched, underground movements emerged as the lifeblood of resistance. These clandestine organizations served not only as safe havens for those marginalized by society but also as incubators for revolutionary ideas that would later fuel Lyra

Thorne's activism. This section delves into the critical role of these underground movements, highlighting their influence on Thorne's development as a leader and their broader implications for the gender rights revolution.

The Fucking Foundation of Resistance

Underground movements in Kyriden were born out of necessity, operating in the shadows of a regime that sought to silence dissent. These groups provided a platform for individuals to express their grievances, share their experiences, and strategize for change. According to theorists like [?], the concept of a "counter-hegemony" became vital in these movements, as they challenged the dominant narratives imposed by the state. Thorne's early involvement with these groups allowed her to grasp the importance of collective action and solidarity among marginalized communities.

The Fucking Network of Support

One of the most significant aspects of underground movements was their ability to create networks of support that transcended geographical and social barriers. Thorne found herself connected to a diverse array of activists, including LGBTQ+ individuals, feminists, and even members of other marginalized ethnic groups. This intersectionality was crucial; as [?] posits, understanding the overlapping systems of oppression enabled Thorne to craft a more inclusive approach to activism.

$$\text{Intersectionality} = \sum_{i=1}^{n} \text{Oppression}_i \qquad (12)$$

This equation represents the cumulative effect of various forms of oppression that individuals face, emphasizing the need for a multifaceted approach to resistance.

The Fucking Dissemination of Ideas

The underground movements also played a pivotal role in disseminating revolutionary ideas. Through pamphlets, secret meetings, and coded messages, activists shared information about gender rights, societal injustices, and strategies for protest. Thorne was particularly inspired by the writings of underground theorists who articulated the need for a radical rethinking of gender roles. These texts often drew on feminist theory, such as the works of [?], who argued for the dismantling of patriarchal structures. Thorne's ability to synthesize these ideas into her activism was a defining moment in her journey as a revolutionary leader.

The Fucking Training Grounds for Activism

Moreover, underground movements served as training grounds for activists. Thorne participated in workshops focused on nonviolent protest, civil disobedience, and grassroots organizing. These sessions were crucial in equipping her with the tools necessary to lead effectively. The teachings often included elements of [?]'s theory of nonviolent action, emphasizing the strategic use of nonviolent resistance to undermine oppressive regimes.

$$\text{Nonviolent Action} = \text{Strategic Planning} + \text{Community Mobilization} \quad (13)$$

This equation illustrates the dual components necessary for successful nonviolent resistance, both of which Thorne mastered through her underground training.

The Fucking Catalyst for Change

The underground movements not only shaped Thorne's activism but also acted as catalysts for broader societal change. By fostering a culture of dissent, they inspired individuals across Kyriden to question the status quo. Thorne often recalled her first protest, organized in collaboration with these movements, as a transformative experience that solidified her commitment to the fight for gender equality. The echoes of these early protests reverberated throughout Kyriden, laying the groundwork for the larger gender rights revolution that followed.

The Fucking Legacy of Underground Movements

Ultimately, the underground movements of Kyriden left an indelible mark on Thorne's activism. They provided her with the ideological foundation, strategic skills, and community support necessary to challenge the oppressive structures of her society. As [?] asserts, social movements are often interconnected, and the legacy of these underground groups can be seen in the continued fight for gender rights in Kyriden. Thorne's activism was not an isolated phenomenon; it was part of a larger tapestry of resistance that continues to inspire new generations of activists.

In conclusion, the role of underground movements in shaping Lyra Thorne's activism cannot be overstated. They were the crucibles of resistance where ideas were born, strategies were honed, and alliances were forged. As Thorne emerged as a leader, she carried with her the lessons learned from these movements, ensuring that their spirit of defiance lived on in the ongoing struggle for gender equality in Kyriden.

Early Fucking Protests: How Thorne Began Her Fucking Journey as a Leader in Kyriden's Gender Uprising

Lyra Thorne's journey as a revolutionary leader in Kyriden began amidst a landscape of systemic oppression and gender inequality that permeated every aspect of life. The early fucking protests she organized were not just acts of defiance; they were the spark that ignited a movement, a bold declaration that the marginalized would no longer be silenced. This section delves into the formative protests that marked Thorne's emergence as a leader and the theoretical frameworks that underpin her activism.

Theoretical Foundations of Protest

To understand the significance of Thorne's early protests, we must first consider the theoretical frameworks that inform social movements. One such framework is the **Resource Mobilization Theory**, which posits that the success of social movements depends on the availability of resources, including organizational skills, financial support, and networks of activists. Thorne leveraged her personal experiences and the collective grievances of her community as resources, transforming anger into organized action.

Another relevant theory is the **Framing Theory**, which emphasizes the importance of narrative in mobilizing support. Thorne was adept at framing the struggle for gender rights in Kyriden as not just a fight for women but as a broader human rights issue. This framing attracted a diverse coalition of supporters, amplifying the movement's reach and impact.

The Context of Early Protests

In the oppressive environment of Kyriden, where traditional gender roles were rigidly enforced, Thorne's early protests were acts of radical defiance. The government's draconian measures against any form of dissent created a climate of fear, but it also galvanized the oppressed. Thorne recognized that the first step towards change was to challenge the status quo publicly.

$$\text{Mobilization} = \text{Resources} + \text{Framing} + \text{Collective Identity} \qquad (14)$$

In this equation, *Mobilization* represents the effectiveness of protests, while *Resources* and *Framing* are critical components. Thorne's ability to cultivate a shared *Collective Identity* among participants was vital, as it fostered solidarity and a sense of belonging within the movement.

Key Early Protests and Their Impact

One of the first significant protests led by Thorne occurred at the annual Festival of Tradition, a government-sanctioned event that celebrated the oppressive norms of Kyriden. Thorne and a group of activists infiltrated the festival, armed with banners that boldly proclaimed, "Tradition Does Not Equal Oppression!" This act of civil disobedience was met with hostility from security forces, yet it drew media attention and sparked conversations about gender rights in the public sphere.

Another notable protest took place outside the Ministry of Gender Affairs, where Thorne and her supporters staged a sit-in demanding the repeal of discriminatory laws. This protest utilized **nonviolent resistance**, a strategy grounded in the belief that moral high ground could be achieved through peaceful means. Thorne's commitment to nonviolence was rooted in the teachings of historical figures such as Gandhi and Martin Luther King Jr., who emphasized the power of peaceful protest to effect change.

$$\text{Nonviolent Resistance} = \text{Moral Authority} + \text{Public Sympathy} \qquad (15)$$

Here, *Nonviolent Resistance* is seen as a function of *Moral Authority* gained through ethical conduct and the resulting *Public Sympathy* it generates. Thorne's ability to maintain this moral authority was crucial in garnering widespread support for the movement.

Challenges Faced During Early Protests

Despite the fervor and commitment of Thorne and her supporters, the early protests were fraught with challenges. The government responded with brutal crackdowns, employing tactics such as surveillance, arrests, and intimidation to stifle dissent. Thorne faced personal risks, including threats to her safety and the safety of her family. However, these challenges only fueled her resolve.

The psychological toll of leading such high-stakes protests cannot be underestimated. Thorne often spoke of the emotional burden of witnessing the suffering of her fellow activists. The concept of **Collective Trauma** became apparent as participants grappled with the repercussions of their activism.

Thorne's leadership was vital in creating spaces for healing and solidarity, emphasizing the importance of mental health in the movement.

The Legacy of Early Protests

The early protests organized by Lyra Thorne laid the groundwork for a broader gender rights movement in Kyriden. They highlighted the urgency of the struggle and demonstrated the power of collective action. As Thorne continued to build momentum, her early experiences informed her strategies and approaches to activism.

The success of these protests also sparked a wave of similar actions across Kyriden, as individuals began to recognize their power to effect change. The early fucking protests served as a catalyst, inspiring countless others to join the fight for gender equality.

In conclusion, Thorne's journey as a leader in Kyriden's gender uprising began with early protests that challenged oppressive norms and mobilized the marginalized. By employing effective strategies grounded in theoretical frameworks, she was able to galvanize support and lay the foundation for a revolutionary movement. The legacy of these protests continues to resonate, reminding us that the fight for gender equality is both a personal and collective endeavor.

The Future of Fucking Gender Resistance Movements: Will Thorne's Fucking Early Activism Continue to Inspire New Fucking Fighters?

The legacy of Lyra Thorne's early activism in Kyriden is a testament to the enduring power of resistance movements and their capacity to inspire future generations. As we analyze the potential for Thorne's influence to resonate with new fighters, we must consider several key factors: the socio-political landscape, the evolution of activism strategies, and the role of technology in facilitating these movements.

The Socio-Political Landscape

The socio-political environment in which new activists operate is markedly different from that of Thorne's formative years. While the oppressive structures that Thorne fought against still exist, the advent of global awareness and interconnectedness has reshaped the battlefield. The equation governing the relationship between oppression and resistance can be articulated as:

$$R = f(O, A, T) \tag{16}$$

where R represents resistance, O stands for oppression, A for activism, and T for technology. The function f indicates that as oppression intensifies, activism must adapt and evolve, leveraging technology to amplify its reach and impact.

In the current climate, new fighters can draw from Thorne's strategies while also integrating modern tools such as social media, which allows for instantaneous communication and mobilization. For instance, movements like #MeToo and Black Lives Matter have shown how digital platforms can galvanize support and create a sense of solidarity across vast distances. This modern landscape provides a fertile ground for Thorne's legacy to inspire action, as her early methods of grassroots organizing can be amplified through these digital channels.

Evolving Activism Strategies

Thorne's activism was characterized by its nonviolent approach and emphasis on coalition-building. These strategies remain relevant but must be adapted to contemporary challenges. New fighters can learn from Thorne's emphasis on intersectionality, recognizing that gender oppression does not exist in a vacuum but is intertwined with issues of race, class, and sexuality. The following equation illustrates the importance of intersectionality in activism:

$$I = \sum_{n=1}^{k} C_n \tag{17}$$

where I represents intersectionality, C_n are the various identities that intersect to create unique experiences of oppression, and k is the number of identities considered. By understanding and addressing the complexities of identity, new activists can cultivate a more inclusive movement that resonates with a broader audience.

For example, the recent global protests for climate justice have highlighted the intersection of environmental issues and social justice, echoing Thorne's approach to building coalitions across marginalized groups. By recognizing these connections, new fighters can honor Thorne's legacy while also pushing the boundaries of traditional activism.

The Role of Technology

The rapid evolution of technology presents both opportunities and challenges for new fighters. Thorne's era relied on physical demonstrations and printed materials to spread her message, whereas today's activists can utilize digital tools to enhance their outreach. The integration of technology into activism can be modeled by the following equation:

$$E = T \times A \tag{18}$$

where E represents engagement, T is the technological tools employed, and A is the activism strategy used. This equation suggests that the effectiveness of activism is amplified when technology is effectively integrated into its execution.

For instance, platforms like TikTok have emerged as powerful tools for activism, allowing users to share their messages through creative and engaging content. The viral nature of such platforms can lead to widespread awareness and mobilization, reminiscent of Thorne's ability to rally support through her compelling narrative and charisma.

Moreover, the use of encrypted communication tools allows activists to organize securely, protecting them from state surveillance and repression—an essential evolution given the brutal responses Thorne faced. By adopting these technologies, new fighters can continue the fight for gender rights in a way that is both safe and effective.

Conclusion

In conclusion, the future of gender resistance movements is bright, fueled by the foundation laid by pioneers like Lyra Thorne. Her early activism serves as both a blueprint and an inspiration for new fighters navigating a complex and ever-changing landscape. By understanding the socio-political context, embracing evolving strategies, and leveraging technology, today's activists can ensure that Thorne's legacy not only survives but thrives, igniting a new wave of resistance against gender oppression across Kyriden and beyond. The question is not whether Thorne's activism will inspire future fighters, but rather how they will adapt her lessons to forge their own paths in the ongoing struggle for equality and justice.

The Fucking Turning Point: When Activism Became Revolution

How Kyriden's Fucking Government Crackdown Sparked Thorne's Fucking Shift Toward Revolution

In the oppressive landscape of Kyriden, where the weight of tradition and systemic gender oppression bore down on the marginalized, the government's crackdown served as a catalyst for Lyra Thorne's radical transformation from an activist to a revolutionary leader. The crackdown was not merely a series of isolated incidents; it was an orchestrated campaign of repression designed to silence dissent and maintain the status quo. This section explores the circumstances surrounding this crackdown and how it galvanized Thorne's resolve to escalate her activism into a full-blown revolution.

The Context of Repression

The Kyriden government, a patriarchal regime steeped in archaic traditions, viewed the burgeoning gender rights movement as a direct threat to its authority. The increasing visibility of activists like Thorne, who challenged the oppressive norms, led to a series of brutal retaliatory measures. These included arbitrary arrests, violent dispersal of peaceful protests, and the implementation of draconian laws aimed at stifling free expression. The government's tactics can be understood through the lens of *state repression theory*, which posits that authoritarian regimes often resort to violence and intimidation to suppress opposition (Tilly, 2003).

The government's response to the rising tide of activism was swift and severe. For example, in the summer of 2023, a peaceful demonstration organized by Thorne and her allies was met with a brutal police crackdown, resulting in dozens of injuries and several arrests. This incident, widely publicized and condemned internationally, marked a turning point in Thorne's approach. The violent repression not only heightened public awareness of the injustices faced by gender minorities but also illustrated the lengths to which the government would go to maintain control.

Thorne's Awakening

Faced with the stark realities of state violence, Thorne experienced a profound shift in her understanding of the struggle for gender rights. Initially focused on reformist strategies—advocating for policy changes and engaging in dialogue with government officials—Thorne realized that such approaches were insufficient in the face of systemic oppression. The crackdown revealed the fundamental nature of the conflict: it was not merely a struggle for rights but a fight against an entrenched system that would not yield to peaceful negotiation.

This realization aligns with the concept of *revolutionary consciousness*, which suggests that sustained oppression can lead individuals to recognize the need for radical change (Freire, 1970). Thorne's personal narrative transformed from one of seeking incremental change to embracing the necessity of a revolutionary movement. This shift was not just ideological; it was deeply emotional, driven by a sense of urgency to protect her community from further violence and repression.

Mobilization and Coalition Building

In the wake of the crackdown, Thorne began to mobilize not only gender minorities but also other marginalized groups who had suffered under the government's oppressive regime. Recognizing the power of collective action, she initiated dialogues with activists from various movements, including labor rights, racial justice, and environmental advocacy. This coalition-building was crucial, as it diversified the support base for the gender rights movement and created a united front against the government's repression.

Thorne's strategic shift can be illustrated through the equation of *collective efficacy*:

$$C = \frac{S}{R} \tag{19}$$

Where C represents collective efficacy, S signifies the strength of the coalition formed by various groups, and R denotes the resistance faced from the government. As Thorne united different factions, the collective efficacy increased, leading to more organized and impactful protests.

Escalation of Tactics

The government's crackdown not only solidified Thorne's resolve but also prompted her to escalate her tactics. Nonviolent protests evolved into more assertive actions, including sit-ins, marches, and the occupation of public spaces. These tactics were designed to disrupt the status quo and draw attention to the injustices faced by gender minorities. The shift from passive resistance to active confrontation was a critical development in the movement's trajectory.

In one notable instance, Thorne led a mass demonstration that occupied the central plaza of Kyriden's capital for three days. This event, dubbed the "Fucking

Stand," attracted thousands of participants and garnered international media attention. The government's subsequent attempt to disperse the protesters only fueled further outrage and solidarity among the populace.

Theoretical Implications

Thorne's evolution from activist to revolutionary leader can be understood through the framework of *social movement theory*, which emphasizes the role of political opportunities and mobilizing structures in shaping activism (Tarrow, 1998). The government's crackdown created a political opportunity that Thorne adeptly seized, transforming the movement into a revolutionary force. This shift also reflects the concept of *catalytic leadership*, where a leader responds to crises by mobilizing individuals toward collective action (Heifetz, 1994).

Conclusion

The crackdown by Kyriden's government was not merely a moment of repression; it was a transformative event that propelled Lyra Thorne into the forefront of a revolutionary movement. By recognizing the limitations of reformist strategies and embracing a more radical approach, Thorne galvanized a diverse coalition of marginalized groups, thereby amplifying the struggle for gender rights. This shift marked a critical juncture in Kyriden's gender revolution, setting the stage for a sustained and organized resistance against oppression. As Thorne's journey illustrates, the crucible of state violence can ignite the flames of revolution, forging leaders who are willing to challenge the very foundations of systemic injustice.

The Fucking Birth of a Movement: How Thorne Organized the First Fucking Gender Rights Revolution on Kyriden

The emergence of a revolutionary movement is often rooted in a confluence of societal pressures, personal experiences, and a compelling vision for change. For Lyra Thorne, the catalyst for organizing the first fucking gender rights revolution on Kyriden was a potent mix of oppressive governmental policies, the marginalization of gender minorities, and her unwavering commitment to justice. This section delves into the strategic maneuvers, the theoretical frameworks, and the grassroots mobilization that characterized this historical moment.

Theoretical Framework: Collective Action Theory

To understand how Thorne galvanized a movement, we must first consider the principles of Collective Action Theory. This theory posits that individuals will only engage in collective action when they perceive a shared grievance and believe their participation will lead to meaningful change. Thorne's ability to articulate the collective frustrations of women and gender minorities was crucial in transforming personal grievances into a unified revolutionary agenda.

$$\text{Collective Action} = \text{Shared Grievance} + \text{Belief in Change} \qquad (20)$$

Thorne's mastery of this equation allowed her to resonate deeply with the populace, as she framed the struggle for gender rights not merely as a personal battle but as a collective fight against systemic oppression.

Mobilizing the Masses: Grassroots Organizing

The birth of the movement was marked by Thorne's strategic grassroots organizing. She recognized that to challenge the entrenched power structures of Kyriden, she needed to mobilize a broad coalition of supporters. Thorne began by holding clandestine meetings in safe spaces, where she could speak freely about the injustices faced by gender minorities. These gatherings were not just about sharing stories; they were workshops for empowerment, teaching participants about their rights and the mechanisms of resistance.

- **Community Engagement:** Thorne emphasized the importance of engaging with local communities. By listening to the experiences of marginalized individuals, she was able to tailor her message and rally support.

- **Symbolic Actions:** Thorne organized symbolic actions, such as the "Fucking Silence Breakers" campaign, where participants publicly shared their stories of oppression. This created a powerful narrative that underscored the urgency of the movement.

Building Alliances: Intersectionality in Action

Thorne understood that the struggle for gender rights was inextricably linked to other social justice movements. She actively sought to build alliances with other marginalized groups, including racial minorities, LGBTQ+ activists, and labor unions. This intersectional approach not only broadened the movement's base but also enriched its strategies and goals.

$$\text{Intersectionality} = \text{Gender Rights} + \text{Racial Justice} + \text{Labor Rights} \qquad (21)$$

By framing the movement as a multi-faceted struggle against various forms of oppression, Thorne was able to attract a diverse coalition of supporters who recognized the interconnectedness of their fights.

Strategic Protests: The First Fucking Gender Rights March

The pivotal moment in the birth of the movement was the organization of the first fucking gender rights march, dubbed the "March for Our Fucking Lives." This event was meticulously planned, drawing on the lessons learned from earlier protests and the need for visibility. Thorne utilized social media to spread awareness and gather momentum, ensuring that the message reached not only Kyriden but also garnered international attention.

- **Logistics and Planning:** Thorne coordinated transportation, security, and accommodations for participants, demonstrating her organizational prowess. The march was designed to be inclusive, allowing people from all walks of life to join in solidarity.

- **Media Strategy:** Thorne engaged with local and intergalactic media, ensuring that the march received extensive coverage. This media attention was crucial in amplifying the movement's message and attracting further support.

Confronting Government Repression

As the movement gained traction, so did the government's response. The Kyriden regime, threatened by the burgeoning revolutionary spirit, initiated a brutal crackdown on dissent. Thorne and her allies faced intimidation, arrests, and violence. However, this repression only fueled the fire of resistance.

$$\text{Repression} \rightarrow \text{Resistance} \qquad (22)$$

Thorne's ability to frame government repression as a testament to the movement's significance galvanized supporters. She utilized these challenges to rally more individuals to the cause, emphasizing that their fight was not only for their rights but for the rights of future generations.

The Aftermath: A Movement in Motion

The first fucking gender rights revolution on Kyriden did not end with the march; it marked the beginning of an ongoing struggle. Thorne's leadership inspired a new wave of activists, each taking up the mantle of resistance in their own unique ways. The movement continued to evolve, embracing new tactics and strategies as it faced the complexities of a changing political landscape.

- **Legacy of Activism:** The march laid the groundwork for future protests and initiatives, demonstrating the power of collective action and solidarity.

- **Ongoing Education:** Thorne established educational programs aimed at empowering future activists, ensuring that the movement's principles and strategies were passed down.

In conclusion, the birth of the first fucking gender rights revolution on Kyriden was a multifaceted process that involved strategic organizing, coalition-building, and a fierce response to oppression. Lyra Thorne's vision and determination not only sparked a movement but also created a legacy that would inspire generations to come. The revolution was not just an event; it was the beginning of a profound transformation in the societal fabric of Kyriden, challenging the very foundations of gender oppression.

How Thorne Built Fucking Coalitions with Other Marginalized Fucking Groups

In the tumultuous landscape of Kyriden, where gender oppression was deeply entrenched, Lyra Thorne understood that the fight for gender rights could not be waged in isolation. To amplify the impact of her movement, she strategically sought to build coalitions with other marginalized groups, recognizing that the intersectionality of oppression necessitated a united front. This approach was not only pragmatic but also rooted in the theoretical frameworks of intersectionality and coalition building, which emphasize the importance of solidarity among diverse groups facing systemic injustices.

Theoretical Foundations of Coalition Building

The concept of intersectionality, coined by Kimberlé Crenshaw, posits that individuals experience oppression in varying degrees based on their overlapping identities, including race, gender, sexuality, and class. Thorne's coalition-building efforts were informed by this theory, as she recognized that the struggles of women and gender minorities were inextricably linked to the struggles of other marginalized communities. By fostering alliances, Thorne aimed to create a broader movement that addressed the multifaceted nature of oppression on Kyriden.

$$C = \sum_{i=1}^{n} O_i \qquad (23)$$

Where C represents the coalition's overall strength, and O_i denotes the individual contributions and struggles of each marginalized group involved in the coalition. This equation highlights the idea that the strength of a coalition is greater than the sum of its parts, as collective action can lead to greater visibility and influence.

Identifying Common Goals

Thorne began her coalition-building efforts by identifying common goals with other marginalized groups. For instance, she reached out to the LGBTQ+ community, racial minorities, and the economically disadvantaged, recognizing that these groups faced overlapping challenges. By facilitating dialogue and understanding, Thorne was able to articulate a shared vision of justice that resonated across different demographics.

One notable example of this coalition-building was Thorne's collaboration with the "Kyriden United Front" (KUF), a grassroots organization representing various marginalized communities. Through joint meetings and workshops, Thorne and KUF leaders developed a comprehensive agenda that included demands for gender equality, racial justice, and economic reform. This intersectional approach not only broadened the movement's appeal but also strengthened its legitimacy in the eyes of the public and policymakers.

Creating Safe Spaces for Dialogue

Thorne understood that building coalitions required more than just identifying common goals; it also necessitated creating safe spaces for dialogue among diverse groups. She organized community forums where individuals from different backgrounds could share their experiences and discuss the unique challenges they faced. These forums served as a platform for mutual understanding and respect, allowing participants to recognize the interconnectedness of their struggles.

In one particularly impactful forum, Thorne invited speakers from various backgrounds, including indigenous leaders, LGBTQ+ activists, and labor rights advocates. The event not only fostered solidarity but also highlighted the need for a unified approach to activism. The discussions led to the formation of joint action committees that focused on specific issues, such as healthcare access for marginalized communities and the dismantling of discriminatory laws.

Leveraging Social Media and Technology

In the digital age, Thorne recognized the power of social media as a tool for coalition-building and activism. She utilized platforms like "Kyriden Connect" to amplify the voices of marginalized groups and to coordinate collective actions. By creating hashtags that resonated with various communities, such as #UnitedForEquality and #KyridenSolidarity, Thorne was able to mobilize support and raise awareness about the interconnected struggles faced by different groups.

The use of technology also allowed for the documentation of shared experiences, which Thorne leveraged to create compelling narratives that illustrated the urgency of the coalition's mission. Video testimonials, social media campaigns, and online petitions became integral components of the coalition's strategy, enabling them to reach a wider audience and garner international support.

Challenges in Coalition Building

Despite Thorne's efforts, coalition-building was not without its challenges. One significant issue was the potential for tokenism, where marginalized groups were included in the coalition without genuine engagement or respect for their unique struggles. Thorne was acutely aware of this risk and made it a priority to ensure that all voices were heard and valued within the coalition.

Another challenge was the differing priorities and strategies among coalition members. For instance, while the LGBTQ+ community might prioritize issues related to marriage equality, other groups may focus on economic justice or anti-racism initiatives. Thorne navigated these differences by emphasizing the importance of a unified message while allowing space for individual group agendas to coexist within the broader framework of the coalition.

Case Studies of Successful Coalitions

Several case studies illustrate the effectiveness of Thorne's coalition-building efforts. One notable success was the "March for Equality," a large-scale protest that united thousands of individuals from various marginalized groups. The event not only raised awareness about gender rights but also highlighted the intersections of race, class, and sexuality. By showcasing the diverse faces of the movement, Thorne was able to draw national attention to the cause.

Another example was the "Kyriden Alliance for Justice," which brought together environmental activists, labor unions, and gender rights advocates. This coalition successfully lobbied for comprehensive legislation that addressed both environmental sustainability and social justice, demonstrating the power of intersectional advocacy.

Conclusion: The Future of Coalition Building in Kyriden

Lyra Thorne's approach to coalition-building laid the groundwork for a more inclusive and effective movement for gender rights in Kyriden. By embracing intersectionality, fostering dialogue, leveraging technology, and navigating challenges, Thorne demonstrated that solidarity among marginalized groups is essential for creating lasting change. As the movement continues to evolve, Thorne's legacy will undoubtedly inspire future activists to build bridges across communities and to fight for a more just and equitable society for all.

In conclusion, the success of Thorne's coalition-building efforts serves as a powerful reminder that the fight against oppression is most effective when diverse voices come together in solidarity. The future of gender rights activism in Kyriden hinges on the ability to sustain these coalitions and to remain vigilant in the pursuit of justice for all marginalized communities.

The Fucking Government's Response to Thorne's Fucking Uprising: Brutal Repression and Resistance

As Lyra Thorne's movement gained momentum, the government of Kyriden responded with an iron fist, employing brutal tactics to suppress the burgeoning revolution. This section explores the multifaceted strategies of oppression utilized by the state, the theoretical frameworks that underpin these responses, and the resilience of Thorne and her followers in the face of such adversity.

Theoretical Framework: State Repression

To understand the government's response, we can draw upon theories of state repression and social movements. According to Tilly (2004), state repression can be conceptualized as actions taken by authorities to prevent, limit, or disrupt collective action. The government of Kyriden employed a variety of methods to stifle Thorne's uprising, including:

- **Legal Repression**: The introduction of laws specifically targeting protest activities and dissent.

- **Physical Repression**: Use of violence, arrests, and intimidation tactics against activists.

- **Psychological Repression**: Propaganda campaigns aimed at discrediting Thorne and her supporters.

These strategies align with the framework proposed by Davenport (2007), who argues that state repression is often a response to perceived threats to the status quo, particularly when movements challenge deeply entrenched social norms.

Brutal Tactics Employed by the Kyriden Government

The Kyriden government's response was marked by several brutal tactics designed to instill fear and dissuade participation in the uprising.

1. **Mass Arrests**: Following a series of protests led by Thorne, the government launched a crackdown that resulted in the arrest of thousands of activists. Reports indicated that these arrests were often arbitrary, with many individuals detained without charges.

2. **Violent Suppression**: Law enforcement agencies were given orders to use excessive force against demonstrators. Eyewitness accounts detailed instances of brutality, including beatings and the use of live ammunition against peaceful protesters. This violence was not just a tactic of suppression but also a means of sending a clear message to potential supporters of the movement.

3. **Surveillance and Intimidation**: The state deployed advanced surveillance technologies to monitor activists. This included the use of drones and facial recognition software to identify and track participants in protests. Activists reported receiving threats and harassment from government agents, creating a climate of fear that stifled dissent.

4. **Censorship and Propaganda**: The government controlled media narratives surrounding the uprising, portraying Thorne and her supporters as violent extremists. State-run media outlets disseminated propaganda that framed the movement as a threat to national security, attempting to delegitimize the fight for gender rights in the eyes of the public.

Resistance and Resilience of Thorne's Movement

Despite the brutal repression, Thorne's movement demonstrated remarkable resilience. Drawing on theories of collective action, particularly the resource mobilization theory (McCarthy and Zald, 1977), we can analyze how the movement adapted to the oppressive environment.

- **Decentralized Leadership**: Thorne emphasized the importance of decentralized leadership structures, enabling local groups to organize independently while maintaining a unified message. This approach mitigated the impact of targeted arrests on the movement's overall effectiveness.

- **Use of Technology**: Activists utilized encrypted communication platforms to coordinate actions and share information, evading government surveillance. Social media became a vital tool for mobilization, allowing the movement to spread its message beyond Kyriden's borders and garner international support.

- **Solidarity Networks**: Thorne forged alliances with other marginalized groups, creating a broad coalition that strengthened the movement's resilience. This intersectional approach not only amplified their collective voice but also provided additional resources and support in the face of repression.

Case Studies of Resistance

Several notable instances exemplify the resistance of Thorne's movement against government repression:

- **The Night of the Broken Chains**: On a fateful night, activists staged a massive protest in the capital, demanding the release of political prisoners. Despite facing violent opposition, the protest successfully drew international attention, leading to widespread condemnation of the Kyriden government's actions.

- **The Underground Network**: In response to mass arrests, Thorne and her supporters established an underground network to protect activists and provide legal assistance. This network operated in secrecy, demonstrating the adaptability and resourcefulness of the movement in the face of state repression.

- **International Solidarity Actions**: As news of the government's brutality spread, global solidarity actions emerged. Activists from around the galaxy organized demonstrations and campaigns to pressure the Kyriden government, showcasing the power of international advocacy in supporting local movements.

Conclusion: The Ongoing Struggle Against Repression

The government's brutal response to Thorne's uprising illustrates the lengths to which oppressive regimes will go to maintain control. However, the resilience and resourcefulness of Thorne and her supporters highlight the enduring spirit of resistance. As the movement continues to evolve, the interplay between state repression and grassroots activism remains a critical area of study, offering insights into the dynamics of social change in repressive environments.

In summary, the government of Kyriden's reaction to Thorne's uprising was characterized by brutal repression and strategic resistance. While the state sought to quash the movement through violence and intimidation, Thorne's leadership and the solidarity of her supporters created a formidable force for change, challenging the very foundations of gender oppression on Kyriden.

The Future of Kyriden's Fucking Gender Revolution: Will Thorne's Fucking Struggles Create Long-Term Fucking Change?

The legacy of Lyra Thorne and her indomitable spirit in the fight against gender oppression in Kyriden raises critical questions about the sustainability and long-term impact of her revolutionary efforts. As we reflect on the trajectory of the gender revolution ignited by Thorne, we must consider several theoretical frameworks and practical realities that will shape the future of gender rights activism in Kyriden.

Theoretical Frameworks for Understanding Long-Term Change

To assess the potential for lasting change, we can apply the *Social Movement Theory*, which posits that movements require certain conditions to achieve significant change. According to Tilly and Tarrow (2015), successful movements often rely on three key factors: political opportunities, mobilizing structures, and framing processes.

Long-Term Change $= f$(Political Opportunities, Mobilizing Structures, Framing Proce

(24)

In Kyriden, the political landscape is gradually shifting, with increasing opportunities for dialogue between the government and marginalized communities, primarily due to Thorne's relentless advocacy. However, the sustainability of these opportunities remains contingent on the political will of those in power, which can be unpredictable.

Challenges to Sustaining Momentum

Despite the progress made, several challenges threaten the longevity of Kyriden's gender revolution:

+ **Government Repression:** The Kyriden government has historically responded to dissent with brutal repression. The potential for a backlash against activists remains high, as evidenced by recent crackdowns on protests. This repression can stifle the movement and deter new activists from joining the cause.

+ **Internal Divisions:** As Thorne's movement gained traction, it attracted a diverse coalition of supporters. However, differing priorities among these groups can lead to fragmentation. The challenge lies in maintaining unity while respecting the unique needs of various marginalized communities.

+ **Resource Allocation:** Activism requires resources—financial, human, and technological. The future of the movement depends on sustained funding and support from both local and international allies. Without adequate resources, grassroots efforts may falter.

Examples of Potential Long-Term Change

Despite these challenges, there are promising indicators that Thorne's struggles may indeed create long-term change:

+ **Legal Reforms:** The introduction of new policies aimed at protecting gender rights in Kyriden can be traced back to Thorne's activism. For example, the recent Gender Equality Act, inspired by her efforts, mandates equal representation in government and provides protections against gender-based violence. This legislation marks a significant step toward institutionalizing gender equality.

+ **Cultural Shifts:** Thorne's movement has sparked a broader cultural conversation about gender identity and rights. The visibility of LGBTQ+

issues in Kyriden has increased, leading to a shift in public opinion. This cultural change is crucial for fostering an environment where gender equality can thrive.

+ **Intergalactic Solidarity:** Thorne's influence has transcended Kyriden, inspiring movements across the galaxy. The establishment of intergalactic coalitions has provided additional resources and support, amplifying the voices of Kyriden's activists and creating a network of solidarity that strengthens their resolve.

Conclusion: The Path Forward

In conclusion, while the future of Kyriden's gender revolution remains uncertain, Thorne's struggles have laid a crucial foundation for potential long-term change. The interplay of political opportunities, mobilizing structures, and cultural shifts will determine the movement's trajectory. As activists continue to navigate the complexities of oppression and resistance, the legacy of Lyra Thorne serves as both a beacon of hope and a reminder of the work that still lies ahead.

The question remains: will the seeds sown by Thorne's tireless efforts blossom into a sustainable movement for gender equality, or will they wither under the weight of systemic oppression? Only time will tell, but one thing is certain: the fight for gender rights in Kyriden is far from over, and the spirit of resistance will continue to echo through the hearts of those who dare to challenge the status quo.

Lyra Thorne's Fucking Leadership in the Gender Revolution

The Fucking Strategies That Made Lyra Thorne a Fucking Revolutionary Leader

How Thorne Used Fucking Nonviolent Protest and Civil Fucking Disobedience to Fucking Challenge Kyriden's Government

In the heart of Kyriden, where the air was thick with oppression and the weight of tradition bore down on the spirits of the marginalized, Lyra Thorne emerged as a beacon of hope. She harnessed the power of nonviolent protest and civil disobedience, crafting a revolutionary strategy that would not only challenge the repressive regime but also inspire a movement that rippled through the very fabric of Kyridenese society.

Theoretical Foundations of Nonviolent Protest

The philosophy of nonviolent resistance has deep roots, drawing from the teachings of historical figures such as Mahatma Gandhi and Martin Luther King Jr. Thorne's approach was heavily influenced by these ideologies, which emphasized the moral high ground achieved through peaceful protest. The fundamental principle can be expressed in the following equation:

$$P = \frac{R}{C} \tag{25}$$

where P represents the effectiveness of protest, R is the level of public resonance, and C is the cost of participation. Thorne understood that by minimizing the cost of participation—through peaceful means—she could maximize public resonance, thereby amplifying the movement's impact.

Strategies of Nonviolent Protest

Thorne's methodology involved a series of carefully orchestrated protests that utilized various forms of nonviolent action, including marches, sit-ins, and symbolic demonstrations. Each event was designed to draw attention to the injustices faced by women and gender minorities in Kyriden. For instance, during the historic "March of the Broken Chains," thousands of activists, led by Thorne, marched through the capital, symbolically breaking chains that represented their oppression. This event not only garnered significant media attention but also united disparate groups under a common cause.

Civil Disobedience as a Tool for Change

Civil disobedience became a cornerstone of Thorne's strategy. By deliberately violating unjust laws, she aimed to expose the hypocrisy of the Kyridenese government. One notable instance was the "Day of Defiance," where activists occupied government buildings, refusing to leave until their demands for gender equality were met. This act of defiance was rooted in the belief that laws upholding systemic oppression were inherently illegitimate.

$$D = \sum_{i=1}^{n} (E_i \cdot I_i) \tag{26}$$

where D represents the overall impact of civil disobedience, E_i is the effectiveness of each act, and I_i is the intensity of public engagement. Thorne meticulously planned each act of civil disobedience to ensure that it resonated deeply with the public, thereby maximizing its impact.

Challenges Faced by Thorne and Her Movement

Despite the moral clarity of nonviolent protest, Thorne and her followers faced significant challenges. The Kyridenese government, threatened by the rising tide of dissent, responded with brutal crackdowns. Activists were met with violence, and many were imprisoned. Thorne herself faced numerous arrests, yet each act of repression only fueled the movement's resolve.

The psychological toll on the activists was immense. Thorne recognized the need for mental resilience and community support. She initiated workshops focusing on emotional well-being and collective healing, acknowledging that the fight for justice was as much about mental fortitude as it was about physical presence.

Case Studies of Nonviolent Actions

Several key events exemplified Thorne's successful use of nonviolent protest and civil disobedience. One such event was the "Silent Vigil," where participants stood in silence for hours in front of government buildings, holding signs that read "We Will Not Be Silent." This powerful visual representation of resistance drew widespread media coverage and public sympathy, demonstrating the effectiveness of silent protest as a means of challenging authority.

Another significant action was the "Rainbow Flash Mob," where activists spontaneously gathered in public spaces, wearing colors representing the LGBTQ+ pride flag, dancing, and chanting slogans of equality. This event highlighted the joy and resilience of the community, breaking the narrative of oppression and instilling a sense of hope among participants and onlookers alike.

The Future of Nonviolent Resistance in Kyriden

Thorne's legacy of nonviolent protest and civil disobedience has left an indelible mark on Kyriden. As the movement continues to evolve, the principles of nonviolence remain a guiding force. Activists inspired by Thorne's methods are now exploring innovative forms of protest, including digital activism and art-based resistance, to adapt to the changing landscape of oppression.

In conclusion, Lyra Thorne's strategic use of nonviolent protest and civil disobedience not only challenged the oppressive structures of Kyriden but also laid the groundwork for future generations of activists. Her unwavering commitment to peaceful resistance serves as a powerful reminder that the fight for justice can be waged without resorting to violence, and that true change often emerges from the courage to stand firm in the face of adversity.

Case Studies: The Fucking Protests, Demonstrations, and Fucking Advocacy Actions Led by Thorne

In the heart of Kyriden, where the air crackled with the tension of oppression, Lyra Thorne emerged as a beacon of hope. Her journey from obscurity to revolutionary icon is marked by a series of protests and demonstrations that not only challenged the status quo but also redefined the very fabric of gender rights activism. This section delves into the fucking protests, demonstrations, and advocacy actions led by Thorne, examining their impact, strategies, and theoretical underpinnings.

The Fucking March for Equality

One of the most significant events in Thorne's activism was the **March for Equality**, held in the capital city of Kyriden. This protest drew thousands of participants, a diverse tapestry of individuals united under a common cause: the demand for gender equality. The march was meticulously organized, with Thorne employing a decentralized structure that empowered local leaders to take charge of their sections. This approach not only fostered a sense of ownership among participants but also minimized the risk of government infiltration, a common tactic used by the oppressive regime to stifle dissent.

Theoretical frameworks such as *Collective Identity Theory* played a crucial role in the success of this protest. By promoting a shared identity among participants, Thorne was able to galvanize support and create a powerful narrative that resonated across different demographics. The slogan, *"We Are All Fucking Equal!"*, became a rallying cry that transcended individual grievances, uniting people in their fight against systemic oppression.

The Fucking Sit-In at the Ministry of Gender Affairs

In a bold move that demonstrated her commitment to nonviolent resistance, Thorne led a **Sit-In at the Ministry of Gender Affairs**. This action was strategically chosen to disrupt the bureaucratic machinery that upheld gender discrimination. Participants occupied the ministry's lobby, demanding immediate reforms to discriminatory policies. The sit-in lasted for three days, during which activists faced intimidation and threats from government officials.

The sit-in exemplified the principles of *Civil Disobedience*, as articulated by theorists like Henry David Thoreau. Thorne's refusal to comply with unjust laws highlighted the moral imperative of resistance. The event garnered significant media attention, bringing national and international awareness to the plight of gender minorities in Kyriden. Thorne's strategic use of social media to document the sit-in and share personal stories of participants further amplified the movement's reach, illustrating the power of digital activism in contemporary protests.

The Fucking Gender Rights Festival

Recognizing the need for community building and solidarity, Thorne organized the **Gender Rights Festival**, a vibrant celebration of diversity and resistance. This festival featured workshops, art installations, and performances that highlighted the struggles and achievements of gender minorities. By creating a space for dialogue and expression, Thorne fostered a sense of belonging among marginalized communities, reinforcing the notion that activism is not solely about protest but also about celebration and resilience.

The festival was rooted in the concept of *Intersectionality*, a term popularized by Kimberlé Crenshaw, which emphasizes the interconnected nature of social categorizations such as race, class, and gender. Thorne's inclusive approach ensured that the festival addressed the unique challenges faced by various groups, creating an environment where everyone felt seen and heard. This intersectional framework not only strengthened the movement but also attracted allies from various social justice causes, amplifying the collective voice for change.

The Fucking Digital Campaign: #KyridenFightsBack

In an age dominated by technology, Thorne harnessed the power of social media through the digital campaign **#KyridenFightsBack**. This campaign aimed to raise awareness about gender-based violence and discrimination, encouraging individuals to share their stories and experiences. Thorne understood the importance of narrative in activism; by providing a platform for personal testimonies, she humanized the struggle for gender rights and fostered empathy among the broader population.

The campaign's success can be analyzed through the lens of *Framing Theory*, which posits that the way issues are presented influences public perception and response. By framing gender oppression as a widespread societal issue rather than an isolated problem, Thorne was able to mobilize a larger audience. The hashtag quickly gained traction, trending across multiple platforms and sparking discussions that extended beyond Kyriden's borders.

The Fucking Legacy of Thorne's Actions

The protests, demonstrations, and advocacy actions led by Lyra Thorne were not merely isolated events; they were interconnected threads woven into the larger tapestry of social change. Each action built upon the last, creating a momentum that propelled the gender rights movement forward. Thorne's ability to adapt her strategies in response to the evolving political landscape demonstrated her resilience and foresight as a leader.

In conclusion, the case studies of Thorne's protests and advocacy actions illustrate the multifaceted approach required to challenge systemic oppression. From grassroots mobilization to digital activism, Thorne's methods were rooted in theoretical frameworks that emphasized collective identity, civil disobedience, and intersectionality. As Kyriden continues to grapple with its gender rights issues, Thorne's legacy serves as a powerful reminder of the potential for change when individuals unite in the face of adversity.

The Fucking Importance of Strategic Fucking Partnerships: How Thorne Built Fucking Alliances with Other Civil Rights Groups

In the tumultuous landscape of Kyriden, where gender oppression was deeply entrenched in societal norms, Lyra Thorne understood that the fight for gender equality could not be won in isolation. This realization led her to forge strategic fucking partnerships with other civil rights groups, creating a coalition that amplified their collective voice and power. The fucking importance of these alliances cannot be overstated; they were instrumental in challenging the oppressive structures that governed their lives.

Theoretical Framework

Strategic partnerships in social movements are often framed through the lens of *resource mobilization theory*. This theory posits that the success of social movements hinges on their ability to mobilize resources—be it people, money, or organizational support. Thorne's alliances with other civil rights organizations allowed her movement to tap into a broader pool of resources, enhancing their capacity to organize protests, disseminate information, and provide legal support to activists facing persecution.

In addition, the *framing theory* played a crucial role in Thorne's partnerships. By aligning the goals of gender rights with those of other marginalized groups—such as racial minorities and LGBTQ+ communities—Thorne was able to create a unified narrative that resonated across diverse populations. This framing not only broadened the movement's appeal but also fostered a sense of shared struggle against oppression.

Challenges and Problems

However, building these fucking alliances was not without challenges. One of the primary issues Thorne faced was the potential for conflicting interests among different groups. For instance, while the LGBTQ+ community sought to address issues of sexual orientation and identity, other marginalized groups might prioritize racial justice or economic inequality. Thorne had to navigate these differences carefully, ensuring that the movement remained inclusive while still focusing on the specific goals of gender rights.

Moreover, the fucking government of Kyriden often sought to exploit divisions within the movement. By portraying the alliances as fractious or disorganized, they aimed to undermine the credibility of Thorne's efforts. To counter this, Thorne employed strategic communication, emphasizing the commonalities between the various groups and the shared goal of dismantling systemic oppression.

Examples of Fucking Alliances

One of the most notable alliances Thorne forged was with the *Kyriden Coalition for Racial Justice*. This coalition, which focused on combating racial discrimination, found common ground with Thorne's gender rights movement. Together, they organized the *Unity March*, a historic event that brought together thousands of protesters from both movements, demonstrating solidarity and shared purpose. The success of this march not only drew national attention to their causes but also highlighted the interconnectedness of various forms of oppression.

Thorne also collaborated with the *Kyriden LGBTQ+ Alliance*, a group focused on the rights of sexual and gender minorities. By working together, they were able to address the unique challenges faced by queer individuals within the broader context of gender oppression. This partnership culminated in the *Pride and Resistance Festival*, an annual event that celebrated diversity while simultaneously advocating for legal reforms to protect LGBTQ+ rights.

The Fucking Impact of Strategic Partnerships

The fucking impact of these strategic partnerships was profound. By uniting different civil rights groups, Thorne was able to create a more robust and resilient movement. The collective strength of these alliances not only increased visibility but also attracted international attention, garnering support from global human rights organizations. This external validation further legitimized Thorne's efforts and provided additional resources for the movement.

Moreover, these partnerships fostered a culture of solidarity that transcended individual struggles. Activists learned from one another, sharing strategies and insights that enriched their collective fight. This cross-pollination of ideas proved essential in developing innovative approaches to activism, such as the use of digital platforms for organizing and advocacy.

Conclusion

In conclusion, Lyra Thorne's ability to build fucking alliances with other civil rights groups was a cornerstone of her revolutionary leadership. By leveraging the strengths of diverse movements, she not only amplified the voice of gender rights activists but also laid the groundwork for a more inclusive and intersectional approach to social justice. The legacy of these strategic partnerships continues to inspire future fucking leaders, reminding them that the fight for equality is strongest when fought together.

$$R = \frac{P + M + O}{C} \tag{27}$$

Where R represents the overall effectiveness of the coalition, P is the pool of people involved, M is the financial resources mobilized, O is the organizational support, and C signifies the challenges faced. Thorne's coalition exemplified how strategic partnerships could maximize resources and overcome obstacles, paving the way for systemic fucking change in Kyriden.

The Fucking Personal Cost of Leadership: How Thorne Balanced Public Fucking Leadership with Fucking Personal Sacrifice

In the tumultuous landscape of Kyriden, where the air crackled with the tension of oppression and the fervor of revolution, Lyra Thorne emerged as a beacon of hope and defiance. Yet, with the weight of leadership came the undeniable burden of personal sacrifice. This section delves into the intricate balance Thorne maintained between her public responsibilities as a revolutionary leader and the personal costs that accompanied her activism.

The Weight of Leadership

Leading a movement is akin to carrying a heavy load on one's shoulders. For Thorne, this load was compounded by the expectations of her followers and the relentless scrutiny of a repressive regime. The theory of *transformational leadership* posits that effective leaders inspire and motivate their followers to achieve extraordinary outcomes. However, the emotional toll of such leadership can be staggering. Thorne often found herself at the intersection of hope and despair, where the victories of her movement were shadowed by the sacrifices she had to make.

The personal sacrifices Thorne endured can be understood through the lens of *role theory*, which suggests that individuals navigate multiple social roles that can conflict with one another. As a public figure, Thorne was expected to be a symbol of strength and resilience. Yet, behind closed doors, she grappled with feelings of isolation, fear, and vulnerability. The pressure to maintain her public persona often left little room for her to process her personal struggles.

The Emotional Toll

The emotional and mental toll of leading the fight for gender equality in a repressive society was profound. Thorne faced threats of violence, imprisonment, and persecution, not only against herself but also against her loved ones. The psychological concept of *vicarious trauma* became a reality for her as she witnessed the suffering of her fellow activists. Each protest that turned violent, each comrade who was arrested, added to the weight of her leadership.

For instance, during the pivotal *March of the Defiant*, where thousands gathered to demand gender rights, Thorne experienced a moment of personal crisis. As she stood on the makeshift stage, rallying the crowd with her impassioned speech, she received news that her childhood friend had been detained by government forces. This moment encapsulated the duality of her existence: the public figure rallying for change while privately mourning the cost of that change.

Balancing Act: Public Persona vs. Personal Life

Thorne's ability to balance her public leadership with her personal life was a constant struggle. The theory of *boundary management* suggests that individuals often negotiate the boundaries between their personal and professional lives. For Thorne, this meant finding ways to compartmentalize her activism while still nurturing her personal relationships.

She often relied on her close-knit circle of fellow activists for emotional support, creating a network that allowed her to share her burdens. This support system was crucial during moments of crisis, where the act of sharing her fears and anxieties became a form of catharsis. However, the very nature of her activism often demanded her time and energy, leaving her little room for personal relationships. The paradox of her situation was evident: the more she fought for the rights of others, the more she risked alienating herself from those she loved.

The Cost of Sacrifice

The sacrifices Thorne made were not merely emotional; they were also tangible. She faced financial instability due to her commitment to activism, often forgoing stable employment to dedicate herself fully to the movement. The concept of *social capital* plays a vital role here, as Thorne leveraged her connections within the movement to secure resources and support. Yet, this came at a cost. The constant fundraising, organizing, and mobilizing left her exhausted, often questioning whether the sacrifices were worth the struggle.

In one poignant example, Thorne organized a fundraising event dubbed *The Gala of Resilience*, which aimed to raise funds for legal defense for imprisoned activists. While the event was a success, drawing attention and resources to the cause, it took a significant toll on Thorne's health. The sleepless nights spent organizing, combined with the emotional strain of seeing her friends face imprisonment, led to a severe burnout that threatened her ability to lead.

The Legacy of Sacrifice

Ultimately, Thorne's journey reflects the broader narrative of activist leadership, where personal sacrifice is often a prerequisite for public success. Her ability to navigate the complexities of leadership, while managing the emotional and personal costs, serves as a powerful testament to the resilience of those who dare to challenge oppression.

In the context of Kyriden's ongoing struggle for gender rights, Thorne's legacy is one of both triumph and tragedy. The sacrifices she made resonate through the movement she built, inspiring future generations of activists to continue the fight for equality. As Thorne herself often stated, *"In the depths of our struggle, we find the strength to rise. Our sacrifices are not in vain; they are the foundation upon which we build our future."*

Through her story, we understand that the path of leadership is fraught with challenges, yet it is also illuminated by the unwavering spirit of those who dare to defy the odds. The balance between public leadership and personal sacrifice is a delicate dance, one that requires courage, resilience, and an unyielding commitment to the cause.

Conclusion

In conclusion, Lyra Thorne's experience illustrates the profound impact of personal sacrifice on leadership within the gender rights movement in Kyriden. The emotional, social, and financial costs she endured serve as a reminder of the heavy toll that activism can take. However, her ability to inspire and mobilize others in the face of adversity underscores the transformative power of leadership. As we reflect on Thorne's journey, we are reminded that every act of defiance carries with it the weight of sacrifice, and it is through this sacrifice that movements for change are born and sustained.

The Future of LGBTQ and Gender Rights Leadership on Kyriden: Will Thorne's Fucking Legacy Continue to Inspire Future Fucking Leaders?

As we look to the future of LGBTQ and gender rights leadership on Kyriden, the question looms large: will Lyra Thorne's fucking legacy continue to inspire future fucking leaders? The answer lies not only in the enduring impact of her activism but also in the structural and cultural shifts occurring within Kyriden's society. To understand this, we must examine several key factors: the institutionalization of LGBTQ rights, the emergence of new leadership styles, and the role of digital activism.

Institutionalization of LGBTQ Rights

Thorne's fucking efforts have undeniably laid the groundwork for the institutionalization of LGBTQ rights in Kyriden. This process involves transforming social movements into recognized entities within the political framework, which can lead to legal reforms and policy changes. The equation that encapsulates this relationship can be represented as:

$$I = f(A, R, C) \tag{28}$$

where I is the level of institutionalization, A is the activism level, R represents the responsiveness of the government, and C denotes the cultural acceptance of LGBTQ rights. Thorne's activism has significantly increased A, putting pressure on the government (R) to respond positively to the demands of marginalized communities. The cultural shift towards acceptance is also evident, as younger generations are more likely to embrace diverse gender identities and sexual orientations.

Emergence of New Leadership Styles

Thorne's revolutionary approach to leadership has opened the door for new styles of activism that are more inclusive and decentralized. Future leaders on Kyriden are likely to adopt collaborative and intersectional strategies, recognizing the interconnectedness of various forms of oppression. This shift can be analyzed through the lens of transformational leadership theory, which emphasizes the importance of inspiring and motivating followers to achieve collective goals.

The equation for transformational leadership can be expressed as:

$$TL = \frac{(V + E + I)}{3} \tag{29}$$

where TL is the effectiveness of transformational leadership, V represents the vision, E is the empathy shown towards marginalized groups, and I denotes the ability to inspire action. Future leaders will need to embody these qualities, ensuring that Thorne's legacy is not just a memory but a living force driving the movement forward.

The Role of Digital Activism

In the age of technology, digital activism plays a crucial role in shaping the future of LGBTQ and gender rights leadership on Kyriden. Social media platforms and online communities provide powerful tools for organizing, mobilizing, and amplifying voices that have historically been silenced. The reach of these platforms allows for rapid dissemination of information and solidarity across vast distances, creating a sense of global community.

The impact of digital activism can be quantified by the equation:

$$D = \frac{(R \times A)}{C} \tag{30}$$

where D is the degree of digital activism, R represents the reach of social media, A is the level of activism generated online, and C denotes the barriers to access. As barriers decrease and reach expands, the potential for mobilization increases, ensuring that Thorne's legacy continues to inspire new generations of activists.

Challenges Ahead

Despite these promising developments, challenges remain. The backlash against LGBTQ rights in various parts of the galaxy serves as a reminder that progress can be met with resistance. Future leaders must navigate the complexities of a political landscape that may still harbor oppressive ideologies. This requires resilience, strategic thinking, and the ability to adapt to changing circumstances.

Moreover, the fragmentation of the movement poses another challenge. As new leaders emerge, it is vital that they maintain unity within the LGBTQ and gender rights community. Thorne's ability to build coalitions and foster solidarity among diverse groups must serve as a model for future activists.

Conclusion

In conclusion, while the future of LGBTQ and gender rights leadership on Kyriden is fraught with challenges, the foundation laid by Lyra Thorne's activism provides a powerful source of inspiration. By institutionalizing rights, embracing new leadership styles, leveraging digital activism, and overcoming challenges, future leaders can carry Thorne's fucking legacy forward. The question is not whether her legacy will inspire future leaders, but rather how they will choose to honor it in their fight for equality and justice. As the struggle continues, Thorne's spirit will undoubtedly guide those who dare to defy oppression and strive for a more inclusive Kyriden.

The Fucking Challenges of Leading a Gender Rights Revolution in Kyriden

How Thorne Dealt with Fucking Oppression, Persecution, and Fucking Government Spies

Lyra Thorne's journey through the treacherous landscape of Kyriden's oppressive regime was not just a matter of personal courage; it was a calculated dance of resistance against a system that thrived on fear and control. The oppressive forces she faced were multifaceted, encompassing governmental repression, societal backlash, and the ever-looming threat of surveillance and infiltration by state actors. In this section, we will explore how Thorne navigated these dangers, employing both strategic acumen and grassroots solidarity to forge a path toward liberation.

1. The Nature of Oppression in Kyriden

The government of Kyriden was notorious for its draconian measures aimed at suppressing dissent. The regime employed a range of tactics to maintain control, including censorship, imprisonment, and violence against activists. Thorne recognized that the state's power was rooted in its ability to instill fear among the populace, and she sought to dismantle that fear through both direct action and community engagement.

$$F_{oppression} = \frac{C + V + I}{R} \qquad (31)$$

Where:

+ $F_{oppression}$ is the overall force of oppression felt by the populace,

+ C represents censorship efforts,

+ V stands for violence against dissenters,

+ I indicates imprisonment rates,

+ R is the rate of resistance among the population.

This equation illustrates the balancing act Thorne faced: as resistance R increased, the force of oppression $F_{oppression}$ could be diminished, but at a cost.

2. Strategies for Resistance

Thorne employed several key strategies to counteract oppression, focusing on the power of collective action and the importance of maintaining a decentralized network of activists. One of her most effective tactics was the establishment of underground cells that operated independently yet coordinated efforts to resist governmental control.

+ **Decentralized Networks:** By creating a network of small, autonomous groups, Thorne minimized the risk of infiltration. Each group operated under a different banner, making it difficult for government spies to track their activities.

+ **Information Security:** Thorne emphasized the importance of secure communication methods, utilizing encrypted channels and coded language to protect sensitive information. This allowed activists to organize protests and disseminate information without fear of interception.

+ **Public Awareness Campaigns:** Through art, music, and social media, Thorne raised awareness about the oppressive tactics of the government, turning the spotlight on their actions and rallying public support for the movement.

3. The Role of Solidarity

Thorne understood that isolation was a tool of oppression. By fostering solidarity among various marginalized groups, she was able to create a united front against the regime. This coalition-building was essential for survival and empowerment.

$$S = \sum_{i=1}^{n} G_i \qquad (32)$$

Where:

+ S is the total strength of solidarity,

+ G_i represents each group involved in the coalition.

Thorne's coalition included not only gender rights activists but also labor unions, environmentalists, and other social justice movements. This intersectionality not only broadened the base of support but also made it harder for the government to target any single group without facing backlash from others.

4. Counteracting Government Spies

The presence of government spies posed a significant challenge to Thorne's movement. To counteract this threat, she implemented several counter-surveillance tactics:

+ **Misinformation Campaigns:** Thorne occasionally fed false information to suspected spies, creating confusion and disrupting the government's ability to anticipate activist actions.

+ **Safe Houses:** Activists were encouraged to use safe houses where meetings could be held away from prying eyes. These locations were chosen for their anonymity and security.

+ **Training in Security Practices:** Thorne organized workshops to educate activists on how to recognize and evade surveillance, empowering them to protect themselves and their comrades.

5. The Personal Toll of Activism

Despite her strategic brilliance, Thorne faced immense personal costs. The constant threat of persecution took a toll on her mental health and well-being. The emotional burden of leadership weighed heavily on her, as she grappled with the knowledge that her actions could lead to imprisonment or violence against her and her loved ones.

$$P_{cost} = E + R + S \tag{33}$$

Where:

+ P_{cost} is the personal cost of activism,

+ E represents emotional strain,

+ R stands for risks faced,

+ S is the social isolation experienced.

Thorne's resilience in the face of these challenges not only inspired her followers but also highlighted the human cost of the fight for justice.

Conclusion

Lyra Thorne's approach to dealing with oppression, persecution, and government spies was a testament to her strategic mind and indomitable spirit. By fostering solidarity, employing counter-surveillance tactics, and maintaining a focus on grassroots mobilization, she was able to carve out a space for resistance in a repressive environment. Her legacy serves as a blueprint for future generations of activists facing similar struggles, reminding us that even in the darkest times, the light of resistance can shine through.

Case Studies: The Fucking Legal and Fucking Political Battles Fought by Thorne and the Gender Rights Movement

In the heart of Kyriden's tumultuous landscape, Lyra Thorne emerged not just as a figure of resistance, but as a strategic mastermind navigating the treacherous waters of legal and political battles. This section delves into the key struggles that defined her leadership and the broader gender rights movement, highlighting the theoretical frameworks, the challenges faced, and the victories achieved.

Theoretical Framework: Intersectionality and Legal Resistance

At the core of Thorne's approach was the theory of intersectionality, which posits that various forms of oppression—such as gender, race, class, and sexuality—are interconnected and cannot be examined separately. This framework guided Thorne's understanding of the legal landscape in Kyriden, where laws were not only discriminatory but also deeply entrenched in a patriarchal system. Thorne's battles were not merely about gender rights; they were about dismantling a complex web of oppression that affected all marginalized groups.

Case Study 1: The Landmark Gender Equality Act

One of the most significant legal battles fought by Thorne and her allies was the push for the Gender Equality Act (GEA), which aimed to eliminate discriminatory practices in employment, education, and healthcare. The GEA was introduced in response to widespread protests and advocacy efforts led by Thorne, who utilized nonviolent civil disobedience to draw attention to the injustices faced by women and gender minorities.

$$\text{Legal Impact} = \text{Public Pressure} \times \text{Coalition Building} \tag{34}$$

The equation above illustrates the relationship between public pressure generated through protests and the effectiveness of coalition-building with other marginalized groups. Thorne's ability to unite various factions—such as LGBTQ+ activists, labor unions, and racial justice organizations—was crucial in amplifying the demand for the GEA.

Challenges Faced: Government Repression and Legal Barriers

The path to the GEA was fraught with challenges. The Kyriden government responded to Thorne's activism with brutal crackdowns, employing tactics such as surveillance, arrests, and legal intimidation. Thorne herself faced multiple arrests, yet each incident only fueled her resolve.

$$\text{Resistance} = \text{Oppression} + \text{Solidarity} \tag{35}$$

This equation captures the paradox of Thorne's struggle: as oppression intensified, so did the solidarity among various activist groups. The government's repression inadvertently galvanized support for the GEA, leading to increased public demonstrations and media coverage.

Case Study 2: The Right to Protest Movement

In addition to the GEA, Thorne spearheaded the Right to Protest Movement, which aimed to secure legal protections for peaceful demonstrators. This movement was vital in a society where dissent was often met with violence and legal repercussions. Thorne organized a series of high-profile protests, strategically timing them to coincide with governmental meetings and public holidays to maximize visibility.

$$\text{Visibility} = \text{Timing} + \text{Media Engagement} \qquad (36)$$

The equation above emphasizes the importance of timing and media engagement in activism. Thorne's adept use of social media and traditional press allowed her to frame the narrative around the protests, portraying them as essential to the democratic process rather than as acts of defiance.

Legal Outcomes and Political Repercussions

The culmination of Thorne's efforts resulted in significant legal outcomes. The GEA was eventually passed, albeit with compromises that Thorne and her allies had to navigate. The law included provisions for gender-neutral bathrooms and protections against workplace discrimination. However, the passage of the GEA also led to a backlash from conservative factions within Kyriden, who sought to undermine its implementation.

$$\text{Political Backlash} = \text{Legislative Success} \times \text{Opposition Mobilization} \qquad (37)$$

This equation illustrates how legislative success can provoke mobilization from opposing factions, which Thorne had to contend with in the aftermath of the GEA's passage. The opposition's efforts included attempts to repeal the law and discredit Thorne's leadership.

Case Study 3: The Coalition for Comprehensive Reforms

Recognizing the need for sustained change, Thorne helped establish the Coalition for Comprehensive Reforms (CCR), which aimed to address not only gender rights but also issues of racial and economic justice. This coalition became a powerful force in Kyriden's political landscape, advocating for reforms in healthcare, housing, and education.

$$\text{Coalition Strength} = \text{Diversity of Membership} + \text{Shared Goals} \qquad (38)$$

The CCR's strength lay in its diversity and shared goals, allowing it to present a united front against the government's oppressive policies. Thorne's leadership was instrumental in fostering an environment where different voices could be heard and valued.

Conclusion: The Ongoing Struggle

Lyra Thorne's legal and political battles exemplify the complexities of fighting for gender rights in a repressive society. Her ability to navigate the intersections of various forms of oppression, mobilize diverse coalitions, and adapt to the changing political landscape has left an indelible mark on Kyriden. As the movement continues to evolve, Thorne's legacy serves as both a beacon of hope and a reminder of the work that remains.

The fight for gender equality in Kyriden is far from over, but Thorne's strategies provide a roadmap for future activists. The lessons learned from her battles will undoubtedly shape the next generation of leaders, ensuring that the struggle for justice and equality continues to resonate across the galaxy.

The Fucking Role of Technology in Spreading Thorne's Fucking Message Across Kyriden

In the age of information, technology emerged as a pivotal tool in the arsenal of Lyra Thorne and her revolutionary movement against gender oppression in Kyriden. The utilization of various technological platforms not only amplified Thorne's message but also fostered a sense of solidarity among marginalized groups. This section explores the multifaceted role technology played in disseminating Thorne's ideals, mobilizing supporters, and creating a resilient network of activists across the planet.

Digital Communication: The Fucking Lifeblood of Activism

The rise of digital communication platforms, such as encrypted messaging apps and social media, allowed Thorne to communicate with her followers efficiently and securely. Unlike traditional media, which was often controlled by the oppressive Kyriden government, these platforms provided a space for unfiltered expression. The use of *Signal* and *Telegram* enabled activists to share strategies, coordinate protests, and disseminate information about government crackdowns without the fear of interception.

$$P_{\text{reach}} = \frac{N_{\text{followers}} \times C_{\text{engagement}}}{T_{\text{time}}} \qquad (39)$$

Where:

- P_{reach} = Potential reach of a message

- $N_{\text{followers}}$ = Number of followers on social media platforms

- $C_{\text{engagement}}$ = Engagement rate of posts (likes, shares, comments)

- T_{time} = Time taken to spread the message

This equation illustrates how Thorne's strategic use of technology maximized the potential reach of her messages, enabling her to mobilize thousands of supporters in a matter of hours.

The Fucking Power of Visual Media

In addition to text-based communication, visual media played a crucial role in spreading Thorne's message. Videos, infographics, and memes became essential tools for raising awareness and galvanizing support. The use of platforms like *Instagram* and *YouTube* allowed Thorne to share powerful narratives that resonated with a broad audience. For example, a viral video showcasing the brutality of government repression during a peaceful protest garnered international attention and support.

$$V_{\text{impact}} = \frac{V_{\text{views}} \times S_{\text{shares}}}{C_{\text{content}}} \qquad (40)$$

Where:

- V_{impact} = Impact of a visual media piece

- V_{views} = Total views of the video

- S_{shares} = Number of times the content was shared

- C_{content} = Complexity of the content (measured by viewer retention)

This formula highlights how visual content can transcend language barriers and communicate complex emotions and realities in a digestible format, making Thorne's message accessible to a wider audience.

Crowdsourcing and Fundraising: The Fucking Financial Backbone

Technology also facilitated the financial support necessary for sustaining the movement. Crowdfunding platforms like *GoFundMe* and *Patreon* allowed supporters to contribute directly to the cause. Thorne's team utilized these platforms to raise funds for legal defenses, protest materials, and community resources.

$$F_{\text{total}} = \sum_{i=1}^{n} D_i \times R_i \tag{41}$$

Where:

- F_{total} = Total funds raised

- D_i = Donation amount from individual i

- R_i = Response rate of individual i (i.e., likelihood of donating)

This equation illustrates the collective power of individual contributions and how technology enabled Thorne to harness the financial resources of her supporters effectively.

The Fucking Challenges of Technology-Driven Activism

Despite the advantages, the reliance on technology also posed significant challenges. The Kyriden government actively monitored digital communications, leading to arrests and persecution of activists. Thorne and her team had to navigate the dangers of surveillance while maintaining their online presence. This necessitated the use of sophisticated encryption tools and anonymity measures to protect their identities and communications.

$$R_{\text{risk}} = \frac{S_{\text{surveillance}} \times E_{\text{exposure}}}{C_{\text{control}}} \tag{42}$$

Where:

- R_{risk} = Risk level associated with digital activism

- $S_{\text{surveillance}}$ = Level of government surveillance

- E_{exposure} = Exposure of activists in the digital space

- C_{control} = Control measures implemented by activists

This equation underscores the precarious balance activists had to maintain between visibility and safety in a repressive environment.

Conclusion: The Fucking Future of Digital Activism

As Thorne's movement evolved, so did the technology that supported it. The lessons learned from Kyriden's struggle highlight the essential role of technology in modern activism. It serves as both a tool for empowerment and a double-edged sword that requires careful navigation. The future of gender rights activism in Kyriden and beyond will undoubtedly continue to rely on technological innovations, challenging activists to adapt and innovate in the face of ongoing oppression.

In summary, the integration of technology into Thorne's activism not only facilitated the spread of her message but also fostered a sense of community and resilience among those fighting for gender equality. As the fight for rights continues, the role of technology will remain crucial in shaping the strategies and successes of future movements.

The Fucking Cracks in the Movement: How Thorne Kept the Fucking Gender Resistance United

In the heart of Kyriden's turbulent landscape of gender resistance, Lyra Thorne faced an array of challenges that threatened to fracture the movement she had painstakingly built. The struggle for gender equality was not merely a battle against an oppressive regime; it was also a complex interplay of diverse identities, agendas, and the inherent vulnerabilities that arose within a marginalized community. This section delves into the fissures that emerged within the movement and how Thorne employed strategic leadership to maintain unity among her comrades.

The Fucking Diversity of the Movement

One of the primary sources of tension within the gender resistance movement was its inherent diversity. The coalition comprised individuals from various backgrounds, including women, non-binary individuals, and members of the LGBTQ+ community, each bringing unique experiences and perspectives to the table. While this diversity was a strength, it also led to disagreements over priorities and methods of activism. For instance, some factions prioritized immediate legislative changes, while others focused on grassroots community organizing.

To address these differences, Thorne implemented a framework of inclusive dialogue. She organized regular forums where activists could voice their concerns and share their experiences. This approach not only fostered a sense of belonging but also encouraged collaboration across different groups. By emphasizing common goals—namely, the dismantling of gender oppression—Thorne was able to bridge the gaps that threatened to divide the movement.

The Fucking Threat of Government Infiltration

As Thorne's movement gained momentum, the Kyriden government responded with increased surveillance and infiltration tactics. Agents were dispatched to sow discord among activists, spreading misinformation and creating divisions. This tactic aimed to exploit existing tensions and undermine the solidarity that Thorne had worked so hard to cultivate.

In response, Thorne and her leadership team adopted a strategy of transparency. They emphasized the importance of trust and communication, encouraging activists to report suspicious activities and engage in open discussions about potential infiltrators. Thorne also initiated training sessions on recognizing and countering government tactics, empowering her fellow activists to remain vigilant and united against external threats.

The Fucking Emotional Toll of Activism

The relentless pressure of activism took a significant emotional toll on many members of the movement. Activists faced harassment, violence, and even imprisonment, leading to burnout and disillusionment. As morale waned, some individuals began to withdraw from the movement, citing exhaustion and fear.

Recognizing the need for emotional support, Thorne established a network of mental health resources for activists. This included access to counseling services, peer support groups, and wellness workshops. By prioritizing the mental health of her comrades, Thorne not only addressed individual needs but also reinforced the collective strength of the movement. Activists were reminded that self-care was not a luxury but a necessity in the fight for justice.

The Fucking Importance of Shared Leadership

Another critical aspect of maintaining unity was Thorne's commitment to shared leadership. Rather than positioning herself as the sole leader, she encouraged a decentralized structure where multiple voices could contribute to decision-making processes. This approach allowed for a broader range of ideas and strategies while fostering a sense of ownership among activists.

For example, during pivotal protests, Thorne would delegate responsibilities to trusted allies, ensuring that everyone had a role to play. This not only empowered individuals but also mitigated the risk of burnout associated with a single leader bearing the weight of the movement. By creating a culture of shared responsibility, Thorne cultivated resilience within the ranks of the gender resistance.

Case Study: The Unity March

A pivotal moment in Thorne's efforts to keep the movement united was the organization of the Unity March, a large-scale demonstration aimed at showcasing solidarity among various factions of the gender resistance. Initially, there were disagreements about the march's messaging and goals, with some groups advocating for a focus on specific issues while others pushed for a more generalized approach.

Thorne convened a series of planning meetings, emphasizing the importance of a unified message. Through collaborative brainstorming sessions, activists were able to articulate a collective vision that encompassed the diverse needs of the movement. The resulting slogan, "Together We Rise: United Against Oppression," resonated with participants and highlighted the strength found in diversity.

On the day of the march, thousands of activists flooded the streets of Kyriden, united in their demand for gender equality. The event not only galvanized support but also reinforced the bonds among participants. Thorne's ability to navigate the complexities of the movement and foster unity was instrumental in demonstrating that, despite their differences, they were all fighting for the same fundamental rights.

The Fucking Future of Unity in the Movement

As Thorne's leadership continued to evolve, she recognized that maintaining unity was an ongoing challenge. The landscape of activism is inherently dynamic, with new issues and voices emerging over time. Thorne understood that the future of the gender resistance movement depended on its ability to adapt and remain inclusive.

To ensure ongoing unity, Thorne initiated regular evaluations of the movement's strategies and goals. These assessments encouraged open feedback and allowed for adjustments in response to changing circumstances. By fostering a culture of continuous improvement, Thorne aimed to keep the movement vibrant and responsive to the needs of its diverse constituents.

In conclusion, the cracks within the gender resistance movement posed significant challenges to Lyra Thorne's leadership. However, through inclusive dialogue, transparency, emotional support, shared leadership, and ongoing evaluation, Thorne was able to keep the movement united. Her ability to navigate these complexities not only solidified her role as a revolutionary leader but also laid the groundwork for a resilient and enduring fight for gender equality on Kyriden.

The Future of Gender Activism in Kyriden: Will Thorne's Fucking Fight Lead to Fucking Legal Reforms?

As the dust settles on the revolutionary fervor ignited by Lyra Thorne, the question looms large: will her fucking fight lead to substantial legal reforms in Kyriden? To answer this, we must navigate the complex landscape of activism, legislation, and societal change. Legal reforms do not occur in a vacuum; they are the culmination of relentless struggle, grassroots mobilization, and the shifting tides of public sentiment.

Theoretical Framework: Social Change and Legal Reform

The relationship between social movements and legal reforms is well-documented in sociological theory. According to *Resource Mobilization Theory*, social movements emerge when groups can effectively mobilize resources—be it financial, human, or informational—to challenge the status quo. In Kyriden, Thorne's movement has exemplified this theory by uniting diverse marginalized groups, pooling resources, and creating a formidable force against systemic oppression.

Moreover, the *Political Process Model* posits that legal reforms are more likely when movements can exploit political opportunities. In Kyriden, the recent governmental repression has created a backlash, which Thorne and her allies can leverage to push for reforms. The key question remains: can they maintain momentum in the face of ongoing resistance?

Current Legal Landscape in Kyriden

Kyriden's legal framework has historically been steeped in patriarchal norms, with laws that explicitly discriminate against women and gender minorities. For instance, laws governing personal status, inheritance, and employment often reflect deep-seated biases. Thorne's activism has already begun to challenge these laws, demanding a reevaluation of their legitimacy and calling for comprehensive reforms.

To illustrate, consider the case of the *Kyriden Gender Equality Act*, a proposed piece of legislation that aims to dismantle discriminatory laws. Thorne's movement has mobilized public support through protests, social media campaigns, and strategic alliances with other civil rights organizations, making it increasingly difficult for lawmakers to ignore the demand for change.

Challenges to Legal Reform

Despite the momentum, several challenges threaten the pathway to legal reform. Firstly, the entrenched interests of conservative factions within Kyriden's government resist any change that threatens their power. These factions often resort to misinformation and fear-mongering to sway public opinion against gender equality initiatives.

Secondly, the lack of representation of women and gender minorities in legislative bodies hampers the progress of reform. As highlighted by the *Feminist Political Theory*, representation is crucial for ensuring that the interests of marginalized groups are adequately addressed. Thorne's movement must prioritize not only legal reforms but also the inclusion of diverse voices in the political process.

Examples of Successful Legal Reforms in Similar Contexts

To envision a future where Thorne's fight leads to legal reforms, we can draw inspiration from global examples. In countries like *Argentina*, the feminist movement successfully advocated for the legalization of abortion through a combination of grassroots activism and strategic lobbying. The *Ni Una Menos* campaign galvanized public support, leading to legislative debates that ultimately shifted the legal landscape.

Similarly, in *South Africa*, the post-apartheid era saw significant legal reforms driven by social movements advocating for gender equality. The *Promotion of Equality and Prevention of Unfair Discrimination Act* is a direct result of sustained activism that challenged systemic inequalities. These examples demonstrate that while the road to legal reform is fraught with challenges, it is not insurmountable.

The Role of International Support and Solidarity

International solidarity plays a crucial role in amplifying Thorne's movement and its potential for legal reform. As seen in the *Global Women's March*, transnational networks can provide resources, visibility, and pressure on local governments to enact change. Thorne's movement has already garnered attention from international human rights organizations, which can lend credibility and support to their cause.

Furthermore, the *United Nations* and various intergovernmental organizations have frameworks that advocate for gender equality, offering a platform for Thorne's message. By aligning with global movements, Thorne can strengthen her position and increase the likelihood of legal reforms.

Conclusion: A Path Forward

In conclusion, while the future of gender activism in Kyriden remains uncertain, Lyra Thorne's fucking fight has laid a foundation for potential legal reforms. By leveraging social theories, addressing systemic challenges, drawing on successful global examples, and fostering international solidarity, Thorne and her allies can navigate the complexities of the legal landscape. The journey toward equality is long and arduous, but with unwavering commitment and strategic action, Thorne's movement can indeed lead to the fucking legal reforms that Kyriden desperately needs. The future is not just a possibility; it is a fucking imperative.

The Fucking Personal Cost of Leading the Gender Rights Revolution

The Fucking Risks and Costs of Advocacy

How Lyra Thorne Faced Fucking Imprisonment, Violence, and Fucking Persecution for Leading the Gender Uprising

In the turbulent landscape of Kyriden, where the government's grip on power was as tight as a noose, Lyra Thorne emerged as a beacon of hope for the oppressed. However, with great power comes great fucking risk, and Thorne was no stranger to the brutal consequences of her activism. This section delves into the myriad ways in which she faced fucking imprisonment, violence, and persecution, illuminating the harsh realities of leading a gender uprising in a repressive society.

The Reality of Repression in Kyriden

Kyriden's authoritarian regime was notorious for its violent suppression of dissent. The government employed a range of tactics to maintain control, including censorship, surveillance, and brutal crackdowns on protests. The oppressive atmosphere was compounded by deeply ingrained societal norms that perpetuated gender-based violence and discrimination.

$$P_{\text{oppression}} = \frac{V + I + R}{D} \tag{43}$$

Where: - $P_{\text{oppression}}$ represents the level of oppression faced by activists, - V is the violence inflicted by the state, - I is the instances of imprisonment, - R is the rate of repression tactics used, - D is the determination of activists to resist.

As Thorne rallied the oppressed, the government responded with an uptick in violence. Protesters were often met with tear gas, rubber bullets, and even live ammunition. Thorne herself became a target, embodying the very spirit of resistance that the regime sought to extinguish.

The Brutality of Imprisonment

Imprisonment was a common fate for many activists, and Thorne was no exception. After leading a significant protest demanding equal rights for women and gender minorities, she was arrested on charges of inciting violence. The conditions of her imprisonment were harrowing; she faced overcrowded cells, inadequate medical care, and psychological torture.

$$C_{\text{imprisonment}} = \frac{S + M + P}{T} \qquad (44)$$

Where: - $C_{\text{imprisonment}}$ denotes the conditions of imprisonment, - S represents the severity of physical conditions, - M is the lack of mental health support, - P is the prevalence of punitive measures, - T is the time spent in custody.

Despite the brutality, Thorne utilized her time in prison to strategize and connect with fellow inmates, many of whom were also political prisoners. Her resilience became a source of inspiration, transforming her imprisonment into a powerful narrative of resistance.

Violence as a Tool of State Control

The government's use of violence was not merely reactionary; it was a calculated strategy to instill fear among the populace. Thorne witnessed firsthand the state's brutality during her activism. Friends and fellow protesters were beaten, arrested, and even killed. The pervasive threat of violence was a constant backdrop to her efforts.

$$V_{\text{state}} = \frac{F + A + K}{R} \qquad (45)$$

Where: - V_{state} indicates the level of violence exerted by the state, - F represents the frequency of violent incidents, - A is the number of activists arrested, - K is the number of known fatalities, - R is the resistance level among the populace.

Despite the risks, Thorne's unwavering commitment to the cause galvanized many. She often spoke at underground meetings, rallying supporters to stand firm against the state's intimidation tactics. Her speeches echoed the sentiments of a generation yearning for change, reinforcing the notion that resistance was not only necessary but a moral imperative.

Persecution: A Personal Toll

The personal toll of persecution on Thorne was immense. As the state intensified its campaign against her, she faced relentless harassment, including threats to her life and family. The psychological impact of such persecution is profound and multifaceted, often leading to anxiety, depression, and a sense of isolation.

$$P_{\text{psychological}} = \frac{T + S + I}{R} \tag{46}$$

Where: - $P_{\text{psychological}}$ quantifies the psychological toll, - T is the trauma experienced, - S represents the social isolation, - I is the intensity of threats, - R is the resilience factor of the individual.

Thorne's ability to navigate these challenges was a testament to her strength and resolve. She sought solace in her community, drawing strength from shared experiences and collective struggles. The bonds formed during these trying times became the foundation of the movement, reinforcing the idea that no one fights alone.

The Impact of Thorne's Struggles

Lyra Thorne's experiences of imprisonment, violence, and persecution not only shaped her as a leader but also served to galvanize the movement. Her story became emblematic of the broader struggle for gender rights in Kyriden, inspiring countless others to join the fight. The government's attempts to silence her only amplified her voice, transforming her into a symbol of resistance.

In conclusion, the path of activism is fraught with danger, particularly in a society like Kyriden, where the state employs violence and repression as tools of control. Lyra Thorne's journey through imprisonment, violence, and persecution highlights the sacrifices made by those who dare to challenge the status quo. Her legacy serves as a reminder that the fight for gender equality is not just a struggle for rights but a battle against systemic oppression that transcends borders and time.

Case Studies: The Fucking Personal Fucking Sacrifices Made by Thorne and Fellow Fucking Activists

In the heart of Kyriden, where the oppressive weight of tradition and gender norms loomed large, Lyra Thorne emerged as a beacon of hope and resistance. However, this journey was not without its costs. The path to revolution demanded sacrifices, both personal and collective, from Thorne and her fellow activists. This section delves into the case studies that illustrate the profound personal sacrifices made during the gender rights uprising.

1. The Cost of Imprisonment

One of the most significant sacrifices made by Thorne was her time spent in imprisonment. Following the first major protest organized by her movement, Thorne was arrested alongside numerous activists. The brutal crackdown by the Kyriden government resulted in a series of detentions, where many activists faced harsh conditions. Thorne's imprisonment lasted for six months, during which she endured physical and psychological abuse. The sacrifices made during this time were not only personal but also symbolic, as her continued presence in the movement inspired others to persist in the struggle.

$$\text{Personal Sacrifice} = \text{Time in Imprisonment} + \text{Physical Abuse} + \text{Psychological Impact} \tag{47}$$

This equation illustrates how personal sacrifice is multidimensional, encompassing not just the time lost but also the physical and mental toll of such experiences.

2. The Loss of Relationships

Thorne's commitment to activism came at a high personal cost, particularly in her relationships. Many of her close friends and family struggled to understand her dedication to the movement. In several documented cases, activists like Thorne faced ostracization from their communities. For instance, Thorne's childhood friend, Mira, who initially supported her, eventually distanced herself due to fear of government retaliation. This loss of relationships created an emotional void, leaving Thorne and others to grapple with feelings of isolation.

$$\text{Emotional Cost} = \text{Loss of Relationships} + \text{Isolation} + \text{Fear of Retaliation} \tag{48}$$

This formula emphasizes how emotional costs can compound, leading to a profound sense of loneliness and fear among activists.

3. Financial Struggles

Activism is often a full-time commitment, and for Thorne and her fellow activists, this meant sacrificing stable employment. Many activists were forced to abandon their jobs to dedicate themselves to the movement, leading to financial instability. Thorne's decision to leave her job as a teacher to organize protests illustrates this sacrifice. The financial strain was palpable, with many activists relying on community support and donations to sustain themselves.

$$\text{Financial Sacrifice} = \text{Loss of Income} + \text{Dependence on Donations} \qquad (49)$$

This equation highlights the economic dimensions of activism, revealing how financial sacrifices can impede personal stability.

4. The Toll on Mental Health

The psychological burden of leading a movement in a hostile environment cannot be understated. Activists, including Thorne, often faced anxiety, depression, and PTSD due to the constant threat of violence and persecution. The emotional weight of witnessing the suffering of fellow activists and community members took a significant toll. Thorne openly discussed her struggles with mental health, emphasizing the need for self-care amidst the chaos of activism.

$$\text{Mental Health Toll} = \text{Anxiety} + \text{Depression} + \text{PTSD} \qquad (50)$$

This equation serves to quantify the mental health challenges faced by activists, illustrating the urgent need for support systems within movements.

5. The Impact of Violence

The risk of violence was ever-present for Thorne and her comrades. Many activists faced physical assaults during protests, and some were even targeted for assassination attempts. Thorne herself narrowly escaped a violent attack orchestrated by government agents. The constant threat of violence not only affected the physical safety of activists but also instilled a pervasive sense of fear that could hinder their effectiveness.

$$\text{Risk of Violence} = \text{Physical Assaults} + \text{Assassination Attempts} + \text{Fear} \qquad (51)$$

This equation underscores the multifaceted nature of violence within activism, highlighting how it can create a chilling effect on participation and morale.

6. Conclusion

The personal sacrifices made by Lyra Thorne and her fellow activists reveal the profound costs associated with the fight for gender rights on Kyriden. From imprisonment and loss of relationships to financial struggles and mental health challenges, the journey to revolution is fraught with difficulties. These sacrifices not only shaped the trajectory of the movement but also serve as a testament to the resilience and determination of those who dare to challenge oppression. As Thorne's legacy continues to inspire future generations, it is essential to acknowledge and honor the sacrifices made in the name of justice and equality.

How Lyra Thorne Fucking Balanced Public Fucking Leadership with Personal Fucking Hardships

Lyra Thorne's journey as a revolutionary leader in the fight against gender oppression in Kyriden was not just marked by her public activism but also by the intense personal hardships she faced. Balancing the demands of being a public figure while navigating her own struggles was a complex equation that required both resilience and strategic thinking.

The Duality of Public and Personal Life

In the realm of activism, leaders often find themselves at the intersection of their public personas and private realities. For Thorne, this duality manifested in multiple ways, including the constant threat of violence, the emotional toll of leadership, and the need to maintain a façade of strength amidst personal turmoil. The equation representing this balance can be expressed as:

$$P + H = R \tag{52}$$

Where:

+ P = Public responsibilities (activism, leadership)

+ H = Personal hardships (mental health, safety concerns)

+ R = Resilience (ability to continue fighting)

Thorne's ability to manage this equation was crucial to her effectiveness as a leader. The pressures of public scrutiny often weighed heavily on her, yet she found ways to channel those pressures into her activism.

Mental Health and Emotional Resilience

The emotional toll of leading a movement in a repressive environment cannot be understated. Thorne faced significant mental health challenges, including anxiety and depression, stemming from the constant threat of persecution. To cope, she employed various strategies, including:

- **Mindfulness Practices:** Thorne engaged in meditation and mindfulness to center herself amidst chaos, allowing her to maintain focus on her goals.

- **Support Networks:** Building a strong support network of fellow activists provided her with emotional backing, creating a sense of community that was vital for her mental well-being.

- **Therapeutic Outlets:** Thorne utilized art and writing as forms of expression, helping her process her experiences and communicate her struggles to her followers.

These coping mechanisms not only aided Thorne in her personal life but also enhanced her public leadership by allowing her to connect authentically with her supporters.

Public Image vs. Personal Reality

Maintaining a powerful public image was essential for Thorne, as it inspired others to join the movement. However, this often required her to suppress her vulnerabilities. For instance, during major protests, Thorne would project confidence and strength, rallying the crowd with her powerful speeches. Yet, behind the scenes, she often grappled with self-doubt and fear.

This dichotomy can be illustrated through the concept of *impression management*, where Thorne carefully curated her public persona to align with the expectations of her followers. She understood that her visibility as a leader was a double-edged sword; while it empowered others, it also exposed her to increased scrutiny and personal risk.

The Cost of Leadership

The sacrifices Thorne made for her activism were profound. She often prioritized her public duties over her personal needs, leading to burnout and exhaustion. The pressure to be a constant source of inspiration for her followers meant that she had to compartmentalize her struggles, often at the expense of her health.

For example, during a particularly intense period of protests, Thorne was hospitalized due to stress-related complications. This incident highlighted the severe consequences of neglecting personal well-being in favor of public obligations. It served as a wake-up call, prompting her to reassess her approach to leadership.

Lessons Learned and Future Implications

Thorne's experiences underscore a critical lesson for future leaders in social movements: the importance of self-care and the acknowledgment of personal struggles. Balancing public leadership with personal hardships is not just a personal challenge; it is a systemic issue that needs addressing within activist communities.

Future leaders can learn from Thorne's journey by recognizing that vulnerability can be a source of strength. By sharing their struggles, leaders can foster a culture of openness and support, ultimately strengthening the movement as a whole.

In conclusion, Lyra Thorne's ability to navigate the complexities of public leadership while addressing her personal hardships exemplifies the challenges faced by activists in repressive environments. Her story serves as a powerful reminder that the fight for gender equality is not only a political struggle but also a deeply personal one. As such, the future of gender rights activism in Kyriden—and beyond—will depend on the leaders' ability to balance these competing demands while remaining true to themselves and their mission.

The Fucking Emotional and Mental Toll of Leading the Fucking Fight for Gender Equality in a Fucking Repressive Society

Leading a movement for gender equality in a repressive society like Kyriden is not just a political struggle; it is a deeply personal and emotional journey. The toll it takes on activists like Lyra Thorne can be understood through various psychological theories and frameworks that elucidate the complexities of activism under oppressive conditions.

The Psychological Burden of Activism

Activists often experience a phenomenon known as *vicarious trauma*, which occurs when individuals are exposed to the traumatic experiences of others. For Thorne, hearing the stories of women and gender minorities suffering under systemic oppression served as a constant reminder of the stakes involved in her activism. According to *Figley (1995)*, vicarious trauma can lead to a range of emotional and psychological challenges, including anxiety, depression, and a sense of helplessness.

The *Cognitive Dissonance Theory* posited by *Festinger (1957)* also plays a crucial role in understanding the emotional turmoil faced by activists. As Thorne fought for gender equality, she often encountered a stark contrast between her ideals and the harsh realities of Kyriden's societal norms. This dissonance can lead to significant mental strain, as individuals grapple with the conflict between their beliefs and the oppressive environment they navigate daily.

Isolation and Alienation

Activism can also result in feelings of isolation and alienation. Thorne's commitment to her cause often meant that she had to distance herself from friends and family who did not understand or support her revolutionary ideals. This sense of isolation can be exacerbated by the stigma associated with gender nonconformity in Kyriden, leading to a profound sense of loneliness. Research by *Meyer (2003)* on minority stress highlights how societal stigma can contribute to mental health issues among activists, creating a feedback loop of stress and emotional distress.

Burnout: The Cost of Commitment

Burnout is another significant issue faced by activists, characterized by emotional exhaustion, depersonalization, and a reduced sense of accomplishment. Thorne's relentless pursuit of gender equality often left her feeling drained and overwhelmed. The *Maslach Burnout Inventory* (Maslach & Jackson, 1981) identifies key dimensions of burnout that resonate with Thorne's experiences:

$$Burnout = Emotional\ Exhaustion + Depersonalization + Reduced\ Personal\ Accomplishm \tag{53}$$

As Thorne poured her heart and soul into her activism, she often faced setbacks and failures, which could lead to feelings of inadequacy and despair. The emotional weight of witnessing the suffering of others, combined with the pressures of leadership, created a perfect storm of mental health challenges.

Coping Mechanisms and Resilience

Despite these challenges, Thorne also exemplified resilience, employing various coping mechanisms to navigate her emotional landscape. Research indicates that social support is crucial for activists, providing a buffer against the stresses of activism (Cohen & Wills, 1985). Thorne built a network of allies and fellow activists who shared her vision, allowing her to process her experiences and maintain her mental health.

Mindfulness practices and *self-care* strategies also became integral to Thorne's routine. Engaging in meditation, journaling, and physical exercise helped her manage stress and maintain a sense of balance amid the chaos of her activism. The incorporation of these practices aligns with theories of *positive psychology*, which emphasize the importance of well-being and resilience in the face of adversity (Seligman, 2011).

The Future of Activism and Mental Health

As the fight for gender equality continues in Kyriden and beyond, it is crucial to address the emotional and mental toll on activists. Organizations supporting gender rights must prioritize mental health resources and create supportive environments that foster resilience among leaders like Thorne.

The integration of mental health support into activism can lead to more sustainable movements, ensuring that activists can continue their vital work without sacrificing their well-being. As Thorne's legacy unfolds, it is imperative to recognize that the fight for gender equality is not just a political battle; it is also a deeply personal journey that requires compassion, understanding, and support for those who dare to lead.

In conclusion, the emotional and mental toll of leading the fight for gender equality in a repressive society is profound and multifaceted. Activists like Lyra Thorne embody the struggles, sacrifices, and triumphs of this journey, reminding us that the path to equality is as much about personal resilience as it is about systemic change.

The Future of Gender Rights Activism in Fucking Hostile Environments: Can Lyra Thorne's Fucking Struggles Inspire Others?

The narrative of Lyra Thorne's journey through the treacherous landscape of gender rights activism in Kyriden is not merely a chronicle of personal bravery; it is a powerful testament to the resilience and tenacity required to challenge systemic oppression in hostile environments. As we look to the future of gender rights activism, particularly in regions where such efforts are met with severe backlash, Thorne's struggles offer a blueprint for emerging leaders and activists.

Theoretical Framework

To understand the potential impact of Thorne's legacy, we must delve into the theoretical underpinnings of resistance movements. The **Social Movement Theory** posits that collective action arises when individuals perceive a shared grievance and believe that they can effect change through organized efforts. This theory is particularly relevant in hostile environments where oppression is systemic and deeply entrenched.

The equation that often encapsulates the dynamics of social movements can be expressed as:

$$M = G + A + R \tag{54}$$

Where:

+ M = Movement potential

+ G = Grievance (the shared sense of injustice)

+ A = Agency (the belief in the power to enact change)

+ R = Resources (the availability of support networks, funding, and organizational structures)

Thorne's activism exemplifies this equation. Her ability to galvanize a movement stemmed from the palpable grievances faced by women and gender minorities in Kyriden, her unwavering belief in their agency, and the strategic resources she cultivated through alliances and international support.

Challenges in Hostile Environments

Activists in hostile environments face a unique set of challenges. These include:

+ **State Repression**: Governments often respond to activism with violence, imprisonment, and censorship. Thorne herself faced brutal crackdowns, yet she transformed these challenges into rallying points for her movement.

+ **Cultural Stigmatization**: In societies steeped in traditional gender roles, activists often confront societal backlash that can isolate them from their communities. Thorne's narrative illustrates how she navigated this stigma by fostering a sense of community and solidarity among marginalized groups.

+ **Resource Scarcity**: Limited access to funding, organizational support, and safe spaces can hinder activism. Thorne's success in building coalitions with other marginalized groups provided crucial resources and visibility.

Examples of Resilience and Adaptation

The future of gender rights activism will undoubtedly be shaped by the lessons learned from leaders like Thorne. For instance, the **Black Lives Matter** movement in the United States has utilized social media as a tool for organizing and advocacy, similar to how Thorne employed technology to spread her message across Kyriden. This adaptability highlights the importance of innovation in overcoming barriers.

Furthermore, the **Arab Spring** serves as another example of how grassroots movements can emerge in the face of oppression. Activists utilized social media to coordinate protests and share their narratives, echoing Thorne's strategies of mobilization and communication.

Inspiration for Future Activists

Thorne's legacy is a beacon of hope for future activists operating under oppressive regimes. Her story demonstrates that:

+ **Courage is Contagious**: By standing up against oppression, Thorne inspired countless others to join the fight, illustrating the power of individual courage in sparking collective action.

+ **Solidarity is Strength**: Thorne's ability to forge alliances across various marginalized communities underscores the importance of solidarity in amplifying voices and creating a united front against oppression.

+ **Global Networks Matter**: The international support garnered by Thorne's movement highlights the potential of global solidarity to provide resources, visibility, and legitimacy to local struggles.

Conclusion

As we envision the future of gender rights activism in hostile environments, Lyra Thorne's struggles serve as both a cautionary tale and a source of inspiration. Her journey illustrates that, despite the risks and sacrifices, the fight for gender equality is not only necessary but also achievable. Future activists can draw from her experiences, adapting her strategies to their unique contexts, and continuing the fight against oppression with resilience and determination.

In summary, the future of gender rights activism in hostile environments hinges on the lessons learned from pioneers like Lyra Thorne. By embracing the principles of collective action, adapting to challenges, and fostering solidarity, new generations of activists can carry the torch forward, ensuring that the fight for equality continues to burn brightly in the face of adversity.

The Fucking Role of Allies in Thorne's Fucking Movement

How Thorne Built Fucking Coalitions with Other Social Justice Movements on Kyriden

Lyra Thorne's journey as a revolutionary leader in the fight for gender equality on Kyriden was not a solitary endeavor. It was marked by her strategic ability to build fucking coalitions with other social justice movements, creating a powerful network of resistance against the oppressive structures that governed their lives. This section explores the fucking strategies Thorne employed to forge these alliances, the challenges she faced, and the broader implications of her coalition-building efforts.

Theoretical Framework for Coalition Building

Coalition building in social movements is grounded in several theoretical frameworks, including **resource mobilization theory** and **political process theory**. Resource mobilization theory posits that successful movements depend on the availability of resources—such as money, people, and organizational skills—while political process theory emphasizes the importance of political opportunities and the alignment of various social groups' interests.

In the context of Kyriden, Thorne recognized that the fight for gender rights was intrinsically linked to other forms of oppression, including class struggle, racial inequality, and environmental justice. She understood that a unified front could amplify their collective voices, making the movement more formidable against the state's repression.

Identifying Common Goals

Thorne's first step in building coalitions was identifying common goals with other marginalized groups. She initiated dialogues with leaders of various movements, including:

+ **Labor Movements:** Thorne connected with labor activists who fought against exploitative working conditions. She highlighted how gender oppression in the workplace was a shared concern, as women and gender minorities often faced wage disparities and harassment.

+ **Racial Justice Movements:** Understanding the intersectionality of race and gender, Thorne collaborated with activists advocating for racial equality. She emphasized that the fight against systemic racism was essential for achieving gender justice, as women of color often bore the brunt of both forms of oppression.

+ **Environmental Justice Movements:** Recognizing that environmental degradation disproportionately affects marginalized communities, Thorne allied with environmental activists. Together, they framed gender rights as part of a broader struggle for a sustainable and just society.

Creating a Unified Strategy

Once common goals were established, Thorne facilitated workshops and strategy sessions to create a unified action plan. These sessions focused on developing joint campaigns that highlighted the interconnectedness of their struggles. For instance, during the *Kyriden Unity March*, Thorne orchestrated a massive demonstration that featured speakers from various movements, showcasing the solidarity among diverse groups.

$$\text{Coalition Strength} = \text{Common Goals} + \text{Shared Resources} + \text{Unified Strategy}$$
$$(55)$$

This equation illustrates that the strength of a coalition is directly proportional to the alignment of goals, the pooling of resources, and the coherence of strategic actions.

Challenges in Coalition Building

Despite Thorne's efforts, building coalitions was not without its challenges. One significant hurdle was the differing priorities among groups. For example, while labor activists focused on immediate economic concerns, gender activists sought long-term cultural shifts. Thorne navigated these differences by emphasizing the importance of a multi-issue approach, advocating that economic justice cannot be achieved without gender equality.

Another challenge was the pervasive distrust among various factions, stemming from historical grievances and competition for resources. Thorne addressed this by fostering open communication and transparency, ensuring that all voices were heard and respected in the coalition-building process.

Case Studies of Successful Coalitions

Thorne's coalition-building efforts led to several successful campaigns that exemplified the power of unity:

+ The *Kyriden Women's Labor Rights Coalition:* This coalition brought together gender rights activists and labor unions to advocate for fair wages and safe working conditions. Their joint efforts resulted in significant legal reforms, including the establishment of a minimum wage and protections against workplace harassment.

+ The *Intersectional Justice Forum:* Thorne organized this forum to address the overlapping issues of race, gender, and environmental justice. The forum produced a comprehensive report that influenced policy changes at the governmental level, highlighting the need for an intersectional approach to social justice.

The Role of Allies and Support Networks

Thorne also recognized the importance of allies in her coalition-building efforts. She actively sought partnerships with international organizations and local NGOs that shared a commitment to social justice. These alliances provided essential resources, funding, and visibility for the movement on Kyriden.

Furthermore, Thorne utilized social media platforms to expand her coalition beyond Kyriden's borders. By sharing stories of oppression and resistance, she garnered international attention and support, which in turn strengthened local movements.

The Future of Coalition Building on Kyriden

Thorne's legacy in coalition building serves as a model for future activists on Kyriden and beyond. The lessons learned from her experiences underscore the importance of solidarity, shared goals, and strategic alliances in the fight for social justice. As new movements emerge, the principles of coalition building that Thorne championed will continue to resonate, fostering a culture of collaboration and mutual support among diverse groups.

In conclusion, Lyra Thorne's ability to build fucking coalitions with other social justice movements was a pivotal aspect of her leadership in the gender rights revolution on Kyriden. By identifying common goals, creating unified strategies, overcoming challenges, and leveraging the power of allies, Thorne not only advanced the cause of gender equality but also laid the groundwork for a more inclusive and intersectional approach to social justice activism on the planet.

Case Studies: The Fucking Communities That Joined Thorne in Fighting Fucking Oppression

The fight against gender oppression in Kyriden was not a solitary endeavor; it was a collective uprising that united various communities under a shared vision of equality and justice. This section explores the fucking communities that rallied around Lyra Thorne, showcasing their unique contributions to the struggle against systemic oppression and highlighting the intersections of their identities and experiences.

1. The Fucking Underground Art Collective: Creatives for Change

The Underground Art Collective emerged as a fucking vital force in Kyriden's gender rights movement. Comprised of artists, musicians, and performers, this group utilized the power of art to challenge societal norms and provoke thought. Their motto, *"Art is Resistance,"* encapsulated their mission to create provocative pieces that illuminated the struggles of marginalized communities.

Theory: The collective adopted the principles of *Critical Art Theory*, which posits that art can serve as a catalyst for social change by raising awareness and fostering dialogue.

Example: One notable event was the *"Fucking Voices of the Margins"* exhibition, where artists showcased works that depicted the raw realities of gender oppression. The exhibition not only attracted significant attention but also raised funds for Thorne's movement, demonstrating the potential of art as a tool for activism.

2. The Fucking Labor Coalition: Workers for Equality

The Labor Coalition, a group representing workers across various sectors, played a crucial role in supporting Thorne's fight against gender oppression by advocating for workplace rights and protections for all genders. Their involvement highlighted the intersectionality of class and gender struggles within Kyriden's socio-economic landscape.

Theory: Drawing from *Intersectional Feminism*, the coalition recognized that gender oppression is compounded by economic inequality. They aimed to dismantle the systemic barriers that marginalized individuals faced in the workplace.

Example: The coalition organized a series of strikes dubbed the *"Fucking Equal Pay Uprising,"* demanding equal wages for equal work and better working conditions. Their efforts not only garnered media attention but also galvanized support from other marginalized communities, emphasizing the interconnectedness of their struggles.

3. The Fucking Queer Alliance: United for Visibility

The Queer Alliance, composed of LGBTQ+ individuals and allies, was instrumental in amplifying the voices of gender minorities in Kyriden. They provided a safe space for individuals to share their experiences and mobilized efforts to challenge discriminatory laws and practices.

Theory: The alliance operated under the framework of *Queer Theory*, which critiques the binary understanding of gender and sexuality, advocating for a more inclusive approach to rights and representation.

Example: Their campaign, *"Fucking Visibility Matters,"* aimed to raise awareness about the unique challenges faced by queer individuals, culminating in a massive pride march that attracted thousands. This event not only celebrated queer identities but also served as a powerful statement against oppression, showcasing solidarity with Thorne's movement.

4. The Fucking Indigenous Rights Network: Reclaiming Identity

The Indigenous Rights Network, representing the indigenous populations of Kyriden, joined Thorne's fight by emphasizing the importance of reclaiming cultural identity in the face of colonial and patriarchal oppression. Their involvement underscored the need for an inclusive approach that recognizes the diverse experiences of all marginalized communities.

Theory: Utilizing the principles of *Decolonial Feminism*, the network argued that true liberation must include the reclamation of indigenous identities and practices, which have been historically suppressed.

Example: The network organized the *"Fucking Heritage Festival,"* celebrating indigenous cultures and traditions while raising awareness about the dual oppressions faced by indigenous women and gender minorities. This festival not only fostered community solidarity but also educated the broader population about the importance of cultural preservation in the fight for equality.

5. The Fucking Student Movement: Youth for Change

Young activists from various educational institutions formed a student movement that played a pivotal role in mobilizing support for Thorne's cause. Their passion and energy brought a fresh perspective to the fight against gender oppression, demonstrating the power of youth activism.

Theory: The student movement was influenced by *Youth Activism Theory*, which posits that young people can be powerful agents of change when they are empowered to engage in social justice issues.

Example: The movement organized a nationwide *"Fucking Walkout for Equality,"* where students from schools and universities across Kyriden walked out of classes to demand gender equality and justice. This act of solidarity not only raised awareness but also pressured governmental institutions to address the issues at hand.

Conclusion

The collaboration among these diverse communities exemplified the power of solidarity in the fight against gender oppression. Each group brought its unique strengths and perspectives, enriching the movement and reinforcing the notion that true liberation is achieved through collective action. Lyra Thorne's ability to unite these communities under a common cause not only advanced the fight for gender rights in Kyriden but also set a precedent for future movements across the galaxy. As we reflect on these case studies, it becomes clear that the fucking fight against oppression is not just about one voice; it's about the chorus of many rising together to demand justice.

How Thorne Gained Fucking International Support for the Gender Rights Movement in Kyriden

Lyra Thorne's journey was not just a local uprising; it was a fucking global phenomenon. To understand how Thorne gained fucking international support for the gender rights movement in Kyriden, we need to look at the strategies employed, the networks established, and the significant role of media and technology in amplifying her message.

Building Strategic Alliances

One of the most fucking critical aspects of Thorne's success was her ability to build strategic alliances with international organizations and activists. Thorne recognized early on that to challenge a repressive regime effectively, she needed to forge connections beyond the borders of Kyriden. This involved reaching out to established NGOs, such as the *Global Gender Coalition* and the *Intergalactic Alliance for Human Rights*, which had the resources and networks to provide support.

Thorne attended international conferences, where she shared her experiences and the dire situation in Kyriden. Her compelling narrative resonated with activists worldwide, leading to the formation of coalitions that supported her cause. Thorne's ability to articulate the struggles of gender minorities in Kyriden in a way that was relatable to global audiences was a fucking game-changer.

Harnessing the Power of Social Media

In the age of technology, Thorne understood the importance of social media as a tool for advocacy. She utilized platforms like *Galactic Twitter* and *InstaGalactic* to spread awareness about the gender rights movement in Kyriden. Thorne's team created viral campaigns that highlighted the oppression faced by women and gender minorities, often using the hashtag #KyridenUprising.

The fucking impact of social media was profound. Activists across the galaxy began to share Thorne's posts, leading to a snowball effect that garnered attention from influential figures and organizations. By creating compelling content—videos, infographics, and personal stories—Thorne was able to engage a global audience, turning them into allies in her fight for gender equality.

International Media Coverage

Another significant factor in gaining international support was the role of the media. Thorne's movement attracted the attention of intergalactic news outlets, who covered the protests and the harsh realities faced by activists in Kyriden. Documentaries and news segments highlighted Thorne's leadership and the movement's goals, bringing her story to the forefront of global consciousness.

For instance, a documentary titled *Fighting for Freedom: The Kyriden Gender Revolution* aired on *Galactic News Network*, showcasing the brutal repression faced by Thorne and her supporters. This kind of media exposure not only raised awareness but also pressured Kyriden's government by increasing international scrutiny.

Mobilizing International Protests

Thorne's charisma and leadership inspired activists across the galaxy to organize solidarity protests. These demonstrations took place in major cities, where people carried banners reading *"We Stand with Kyriden"* and *"Gender Rights Are Human Rights"*. The visual impact of these protests, often covered by the media, further amplified Thorne's message.

The international protests served multiple purposes: they raised awareness, showed solidarity, and pressured Kyriden's government to reconsider its oppressive policies. The fucking visual of thousands of people united in support of Thorne's cause sent a powerful message that the world was watching.

Leveraging International Law and Human Rights Frameworks

Thorne also strategically positioned her movement within the frameworks of international law and human rights. By aligning her cause with established human rights norms, she was able to attract the attention of international bodies such as the *Galactic Human Rights Council.*

Thorne and her team submitted reports detailing the violations occurring in Kyriden, framing them within the context of international human rights treaties. This legal strategy not only legitimized her cause but also opened doors for international interventions and support.

Challenges and Backlash

Despite the overwhelming support, Thorne faced significant challenges in her quest for international backing. The Kyriden government, aware of the growing global attention, launched a counter-campaign aimed at discrediting her and her movement. They portrayed Thorne as a radical, claiming that her actions threatened the stability of Kyriden.

In response, Thorne and her allies had to navigate a complex landscape of misinformation and propaganda. They worked tirelessly to counteract these narratives by providing factual information and personal testimonies from those affected by the regime's policies.

Conclusion

Lyra Thorne's ability to gain fucking international support for the gender rights movement in Kyriden was a multifaceted endeavor that involved strategic alliances, effective use of social media, international media coverage, mobilization of global protests, and leveraging legal frameworks. Through her relentless efforts, Thorne transformed a local struggle into a global movement, inspiring countless individuals and organizations to join the fight for gender equality. As the movement continues to grow, Thorne's legacy as a fucking revolutionary leader remains firmly entrenched in the hearts and minds of those who dare to challenge oppression.

The Fucking Power of Intergalactic Fucking Advocacy: How Global Fucking Movements Supported Thorne's Fucking Struggle

In the vast expanse of the cosmos, where countless planets grapple with their own struggles for equality and justice, the intergalactic advocacy surrounding Lyra Thorne's movement on Kyriden emerged as a beacon of hope and solidarity. The interconnectedness of our universe has allowed for the sharing of ideas, strategies, and resources among marginalized groups, enhancing the fight against oppression. This section delves into the profound impact of global movements on Thorne's struggle, highlighting key theories, challenges, and exemplary case studies that illustrate the power of intergalactic solidarity.

Theoretical Framework of Intergalactic Advocacy

At the core of intergalactic advocacy lies the theory of **Transnationalism**, which posits that social movements can transcend national borders, fostering a sense of global citizenship and collective responsibility. This theory emphasizes the importance of networks in mobilizing resources, sharing knowledge, and amplifying voices that are often silenced. In Thorne's case, her movement was not only a local phenomenon but also part of a broader struggle for gender rights across the galaxy.

The equation that encapsulates the essence of this advocacy can be represented as:

$$\text{Global Solidarity} = f(\text{Local Movements, Shared Goals, Resource Exchange})$$

Where: - Global Solidarity represents the collective strength of movements across different planets. - Local Movements refers to the grassroots efforts on Kyriden. - Shared Goals signifies the common objectives of gender equality and human rights. - Resource Exchange denotes the sharing of knowledge, funding, and strategic support.

This framework illustrates how Thorne's fight was bolstered by the solidarity of other movements, creating a ripple effect that resonated across the galaxy.

Challenges Faced by Intergalactic Movements

While the power of intergalactic advocacy was significant, it was not without its challenges. One of the primary issues was the **Cultural Differences** that existed between various movements. Each planet had its own unique context, history, and struggles, which sometimes led to misunderstandings or conflicting priorities. For instance, while Thorne's movement focused heavily on gender equality, other movements may have prioritized issues such as racial justice or environmental sustainability.

Additionally, the **Resource Disparity** posed a significant hurdle. Not all planets had the same level of access to technology, funding, or organizational capacity. This inequality meant that while some movements could mobilize large-scale protests or campaigns, others struggled to gain traction, leading to an imbalance in support for Thorne's cause.

Case Studies of Support for Thorne's Movement

1. **The Galactic Coalition for Gender Rights (GCG):** Formed in response to Thorne's uprising, the GCG was a collective of activists from various planets, including Vortax-7, a world known for its advanced communication technologies. The coalition provided Thorne's movement with critical resources, including digital platforms for organizing protests and disseminating information. Their support enabled the Kyriden movement to reach a wider audience, garnering international attention and solidarity.

2. **The Intergalactic Pride March (IPM):** In a historic demonstration, activists from over thirty planets converged in a massive virtual space to participate in the IPM, showcasing their support for Thorne. This event not only highlighted the shared struggles of LGBTQ+ communities across the galaxy but also raised significant funds for the Kyriden movement. The IPM's success demonstrated the effectiveness of coordinated efforts and the power of collective action.

3. **The Cosmic Fund for Equality (CFE):** Established by intergalactic philanthropists, the CFE provided financial backing to Thorne's movement, allowing for the organization of larger protests and awareness campaigns. This funding was crucial in facilitating legal battles against the oppressive Kyriden government, showcasing the importance of financial resources in sustaining activism.

The Future of Intergalactic Advocacy

As Thorne's movement continues to evolve, the role of intergalactic advocacy remains pivotal. The lessons learned from past collaborations can inform future strategies, fostering a more inclusive and united front against oppression. The importance of building **Inclusive Networks** cannot be overstated; movements must prioritize dialogue and understanding to overcome cultural barriers and align their goals.

Moreover, the potential for **Technological Innovations** in advocacy offers exciting possibilities. As new communication platforms emerge, the ability to mobilize support and share resources across galaxies will only increase. This technological advancement can facilitate real-time collaboration, allowing movements to respond swiftly to challenges and opportunities.

In conclusion, the power of intergalactic advocacy in supporting Lyra Thorne's struggle is a testament to the strength of solidarity in the face of oppression. By harnessing the collective power of movements across the galaxy, Thorne's legacy will continue to inspire future generations of activists, ensuring that the fight for gender equality and justice resonates far beyond the borders of Kyriden.

The Future of International Fucking Solidarity: Will Thorne's Fucking Movement Continue to Gain Global Fucking Attention?

In the age of digital connectivity and global activism, the potential for Lyra Thorne's movement to gain international attention is not just a possibility; it's an imperative. The question remains: will Thorne's fucking movement continue to resonate with activists across the globe? To explore this, we must delve into the multifaceted dynamics of international solidarity, the challenges faced, and the potential pathways for the future.

Theoretical Framework of International Solidarity

International solidarity, as articulated by theorists such as [?], is rooted in the understanding that struggles for justice are interconnected. This interconnectedness is often encapsulated in the equation:

$$S = \sum_{i=1}^{n} J_i$$

where S represents the total solidarity across movements, and J_i denotes individual justice struggles. Thorne's movement can be seen as a critical component of this equation, contributing to a broader tapestry of global activism against gender oppression.

The concept of intersectionality, pioneered by [?], further emphasizes that the experiences of marginalized groups are shaped by overlapping systems of oppression. Thorne's advocacy for gender rights on Kyriden is not an isolated phenomenon; it aligns with the struggles of LGBTQ+ communities worldwide, creating a powerful narrative that can galvanize international support.

Challenges to Global Attention

Despite the potential for widespread support, several challenges threaten the sustainability of Thorne's movement on the international stage:

- **Cultural Misunderstandings:** Activism does not occur in a vacuum. The unique cultural context of Kyriden may not translate seamlessly to other regions, leading to potential misinterpretations of Thorne's goals and methods.

- **Resource Disparities:** Many movements face significant resource constraints. Thorne's movement must navigate the complexities of funding, visibility, and access to global platforms that can amplify its message.

- **Political Backlash:** As Thorne's movement gains traction, it may provoke backlash from conservative factions both locally and globally. Such resistance can undermine solidarity efforts and create divisions among potential allies.

- **Digital Divide:** While technology can enhance global communication, it can also exacerbate inequalities. Not all activists have equal access to digital tools, limiting the reach of Thorne's message.

Examples of Successful International Solidarity

To envision a future where Thorne's movement continues to thrive globally, we can look to successful case studies of international solidarity that have overcome similar challenges.

- **The #MeToo Movement:** Originating in the United States, the #MeToo movement quickly gained international traction, demonstrating the power of shared narratives in uniting activists across borders. Thorne's movement can adopt similar strategies by leveraging social media to create a global dialogue about gender oppression.

+ **The Global Climate Strikes:** Movements like Fridays for Future have shown how localized efforts can resonate on a global scale. By framing gender rights within the context of broader social justice issues, Thorne's movement can attract diverse coalitions that amplify its reach.

+ **The International Women's Strike:** This movement illustrates how coordinated actions can transcend national boundaries. Thorne's movement could benefit from organizing synchronized protests or campaigns that draw attention to gender issues in Kyriden while connecting with global movements.

Pathways for Future Engagement

To ensure that Thorne's movement continues to gain global attention, several strategic pathways can be explored:

+ **Building Alliances:** Establishing partnerships with established global organizations can provide Thorne's movement with the necessary resources and visibility. Collaborations with entities like Amnesty International or Human Rights Watch can amplify its message.

+ **Utilizing Digital Platforms:** Social media campaigns can serve as powerful tools for raising awareness and mobilizing support. Thorne's movement should harness platforms like Twitter, Instagram, and TikTok to share stories, organize events, and engage with a global audience.

+ **Educational Initiatives:** Creating educational content that highlights the intersections of gender rights and other social justice issues can foster a deeper understanding of Thorne's mission. Webinars, online courses, and interactive workshops can engage a diverse audience.

+ **Engaging in Global Discourse:** Actively participating in international forums, conferences, and panels can position Thorne's movement as a key player in the global conversation about gender rights. This visibility can attract allies and resources.

Conclusion

The future of international solidarity for Lyra Thorne's movement hinges on its ability to adapt, connect, and resonate with a global audience. By navigating the challenges of cultural understanding, resource disparities, and political resistance, while also drawing inspiration from successful global movements, Thorne's legacy can continue to inspire and empower activists across the galaxy. The question is not merely whether Thorne's movement will gain attention, but how it will leverage that attention to create lasting change for gender rights on Kyriden and beyond.

Lyra Thorne's Fucking Legacy: Shaping the Future of Gender Rights in Kyriden and Beyond

Thorne's Fucking Impact on Kyriden's Political Fucking Landscape

How Lyra Thorne Fucking Changed the Fucking Course of Gender Rights Advocacy in Kyriden

Lyra Thorne's emergence as a revolutionary figure in Kyriden marked a fucking seismic shift in the landscape of gender rights advocacy. Before her rise, the narrative surrounding gender roles was steeped in tradition and oppression, with women and gender minorities relegated to the margins of society. Thorne's fierce activism and unapologetic approach to challenging the status quo not only galvanized the oppressed but also forced a reevaluation of entrenched societal norms.

At the heart of Thorne's impact was her ability to articulate the lived experiences of those who had been silenced. She employed a narrative framework that drew from the works of feminist theorists such as Judith Butler, whose concept of gender performativity highlighted the constructed nature of gender roles. Thorne's speeches often echoed Butler's assertion that "gender is not something we are, but something we do," emphasizing that the rigid binaries imposed by Kyriden's patriarchal structures were not inherent truths but socially constructed limitations.

$$\text{Gender Identity} = f(\text{Cultural Norms, Personal Experience}) \qquad (56)$$

This equation illustrates that gender identity is a function of both cultural norms and personal experience, a principle that Thorne leveraged to unite individuals across diverse backgrounds in a common struggle for recognition and rights. By framing the fight for gender equality as not just a women's issue but a human rights issue, Thorne expanded the movement's reach and fostered solidarity among various marginalized groups.

One of the critical problems Thorne confronted was the pervasive violence against women and gender minorities, which was institutionalized in Kyriden's legal framework. She highlighted cases of domestic violence, sexual harassment, and systemic discrimination that were often brushed under the rug by authorities. Thorne's advocacy led to the formation of grassroots organizations that provided support and resources to survivors, transforming the narrative from one of victimhood to one of empowerment.

For instance, Thorne initiated the "Fucking Safe Spaces" campaign, which created community-led support networks that not only offered shelter and legal assistance but also educated individuals about their rights. This campaign was rooted in the principles of community organizing as articulated by theorists like Saul Alinsky, who emphasized the importance of building power from the ground up.

$$\text{Community Power} = \text{Collective Action} + \text{Shared Resources} \qquad (57)$$

This equation represents how Thorne's movement harnessed collective action and shared resources to build a formidable force against oppression. By empowering individuals to take charge of their narratives and advocate for their rights, Thorne changed the course of gender rights advocacy in Kyriden, shifting it from passive resistance to active, organized revolution.

Moreover, Thorne's strategic use of social media and technology played a pivotal role in amplifying her message. She understood that in a world increasingly dominated by digital communication, the ability to reach a wider audience was crucial. Thorne's campaigns often went viral, drawing international attention to the struggles faced by Kyriden's gender minorities. This global spotlight not only put pressure on the Kyriden government to respond but also attracted allies from around the galaxy who were inspired by her courage and tenacity.

Thorne's leadership style was characterized by inclusivity and collaboration. She actively sought to build coalitions with other social justice movements, recognizing that the fight for gender rights was interconnected with struggles against racism, classism, and other forms of oppression. By aligning with groups advocating for racial equality and economic justice, Thorne reinforced the idea that true liberation could only be achieved through an intersectional approach.

In conclusion, Lyra Thorne's impact on gender rights advocacy in Kyriden was profound and transformative. Through her fearless leadership, she not only challenged the oppressive structures that governed the lives of women and gender minorities but also inspired a generation of activists to continue the fight for equality. Her legacy is a testament to the power of resistance, the importance of community, and the necessity of challenging societal norms. As Kyriden continues to grapple with its gender issues, Thorne's influence will undoubtedly shape the future of advocacy, ensuring that the fight for justice remains at the forefront of societal change.

Case Studies: The Fucking Legal Reforms, Protests, and Fucking Movements Shaped by Thorne's Fucking Leadership

Lyra Thorne's journey as a revolutionary leader in Kyriden was marked by a series of pivotal legal reforms, protests, and movements that not only challenged the status quo but also reshaped the landscape of gender rights advocacy. This section delves into key case studies that illustrate the profound impact of Thorne's leadership on the fight for gender equality.

1. The Fucking Legal Reforms: A New Dawn for Gender Rights

Under Thorne's leadership, Kyriden witnessed a series of groundbreaking legal reforms that aimed to dismantle the systemic oppression of women and gender minorities. One of the most significant achievements was the enactment of the Gender Equality Act (GEA) of 2045, which was a direct response to the grassroots movements spearheaded by Thorne. The GEA mandated equal pay for equal work, prohibited discrimination based on gender identity, and established comprehensive protections against gender-based violence.

The theoretical framework supporting these reforms can be understood through the lens of intersectionality, as proposed by Kimberlé Crenshaw. Intersectionality emphasizes the interconnectedness of social categorizations such as race, class, and gender, which create overlapping systems of discrimination. Thorne's activism highlighted the necessity of an intersectional approach to legal reform, ensuring that the voices of marginalized groups were not only heard but prioritized.

$$\text{Intersectional Impact} = \sum_{i=1}^{n} \text{Discrimination}_i \times \text{Advocacy}_i \qquad (58)$$

In this equation, Discrimination_i represents the various forms of oppression faced by individuals, while Advocacy_i signifies the efforts made to combat these injustices. Thorne's multifaceted approach to activism resulted in a significant increase in legal protections for all marginalized communities in Kyriden.

2. The Fucking Protests: Mobilizing the Masses

Thorne's ability to mobilize large groups of people was evident during the "March of the Fucking Free" in 2046, which drew over 100,000 participants from across Kyriden. This protest was not just a demonstration; it was a statement of defiance against the oppressive government. Thorne's strategic use of social media and grassroots organizing techniques played a crucial role in galvanizing support.

The protest utilized the principles of nonviolent resistance, as articulated by theorists like Gene Sharp. Sharp's framework outlines the importance of strategic planning, public participation, and psychological warfare in nonviolent movements. Thorne's team meticulously planned the March of the Fucking Free, ensuring that it was inclusive, engaging, and impactful.

$$\text{Movement Impact} = \frac{\text{Participants} \times \text{Media Coverage}}{\text{Government Repression}} \qquad (59)$$

This equation illustrates how the impact of a movement can be amplified by the number of participants and the extent of media coverage while countered by government repression. The March of the Fucking Free was covered extensively in intergalactic news, bringing international attention to the plight of gender minorities in Kyriden.

3. The Fucking Movements: Building Alliances Across Marginalized Groups

Thorne understood that the fight for gender rights could not be isolated; it had to be part of a broader struggle for social justice. One of her most significant achievements was the formation of the Coalition for Inclusive Rights (CIR) in 2047, which united various marginalized groups, including LGBTQ+ activists, racial minorities, and labor unions. This coalition was instrumental in advocating for comprehensive reforms and amplifying the voices of the oppressed.

The coalition's approach aligns with the theory of collective efficacy, which posits that groups with shared goals can achieve more significant outcomes than individuals acting alone. Thorne's leadership fostered a sense of solidarity among diverse groups, leading to a series of successful campaigns that culminated in the "Fucking Equality Summit" of 2048.

$$\text{Collective Efficacy} = \text{Group Cohesion} \times \text{Shared Goals} \qquad (60)$$

In this context, group cohesion refers to the strength of the relationships among coalition members, while shared goals signify the common objectives that unite them. Thorne's ability to cultivate both elements was crucial in driving the coalition's success.

4. The Fucking Challenges and Triumphs of Leadership

Despite these successes, Thorne faced significant challenges, including government crackdowns, misinformation campaigns, and internal divisions within the movement. The government's response to the protests often involved brutal repression, which Thorne and her allies countered with resilience and strategic nonviolent resistance.

One notable instance was the "Night of the Fucking Silence" in 2049, where activists staged a silent protest outside the government headquarters to symbolize the silencing of marginalized voices. This event not only drew national attention but also highlighted the government's oppressive tactics, ultimately leading to a public outcry for reform.

Theoretical insights from social movement theory underscore the importance of framing and narrative in activism. Thorne's ability to craft compelling narratives around the struggles of gender minorities helped to shift public perception and garner widespread support.

$$\text{Public Support} = \text{Narrative Strength} \times \text{Media Engagement} \qquad (61)$$

In this equation, narrative strength refers to the effectiveness of the stories told by activists, while media engagement indicates how well these narratives are disseminated through various channels. Thorne's adeptness at utilizing both elements significantly contributed to the movement's momentum.

5. Conclusion: The Fucking Legacy of Thorne's Leadership

The legal reforms, protests, and movements shaped by Lyra Thorne's leadership have left an indelible mark on Kyriden's political landscape. Her ability to galvanize support, build coalitions, and navigate the complexities of activism has not only advanced gender rights but has also inspired a new generation of activists.

As we look to the future, the question remains: will Thorne's fucking legacy continue to inspire systemic fucking change? The answer lies in the ongoing struggles of those who carry her torch, fighting for a world free from oppression. The case studies outlined in this section serve as a testament to the power of collective action and the enduring impact of visionary leadership in the fight for justice.

How Thorne Fucking Transformed the Public Fucking Conversation About Gender Rights in Kyriden

Lyra Thorne's rise as a revolutionary leader in Kyriden was not just a response to the systemic gender oppression that plagued the planet; it was also a catalyst for a seismic shift in the public fucking conversation about gender rights. In a society where traditional norms dictated the roles and behaviors of individuals based on their gender, Thorne's unapologetic activism challenged these entrenched beliefs and sparked a broader dialogue about identity, equality, and rights.

Theoretical Framework: Social Constructivism and Gender Identity

To understand Thorne's impact, we must examine the theoretical underpinnings of gender as a social construct. Social constructivism posits that societal norms and roles are not inherent but are created and maintained through social processes. Thorne's activism illuminated this concept, arguing that gender roles were not merely natural phenomena but rather constructs that could be deconstructed and redefined. This perspective aligns with Judith Butler's theory of gender performativity, which suggests that gender is an ongoing performance rather than a fixed identity. Thorne's public demonstrations and speeches often echoed Butler's sentiments, emphasizing that the performance of gender could be contested and reshaped.

The Role of Media in Amplifying Thorne's Message

Thorne understood the power of media in shaping public discourse. By leveraging social media platforms, traditional news outlets, and even underground publications, she disseminated her message far and wide. The use of hashtags like #BreakTheChains and #KyridenEquality not only galvanized support but also created a shared digital space for discourse. This approach transformed the narrative around gender rights from a niche concern to a mainstream topic.

For instance, during the pivotal "March for Equality" in 2043, Thorne utilized live-streaming technology to broadcast the event globally, allowing those who couldn't attend to participate virtually. This tactic not only increased visibility but also fostered a sense of solidarity among disparate groups, creating a unified front against oppression. The event was marked by powerful speeches that challenged the status quo, such as Thorne's declaration: "We are not defined by the boxes they put us in; we are the architects of our own fucking identities!"

Public Engagement and Grassroots Mobilization

Thorne's ability to transform the conversation also stemmed from her grassroots mobilization efforts. She organized community forums and workshops that invited open discussions about gender identity and rights. These events were designed to empower individuals to share their personal experiences, thus humanizing the abstract concept of gender rights. By creating safe spaces for dialogue, Thorne encouraged participants to challenge their own beliefs and biases, fostering a culture of acceptance and understanding.

One notable example was the "Voices of Kyriden" series, where individuals from diverse backgrounds shared their stories of gender oppression and resilience. This initiative not only highlighted the multifaceted nature of gender issues but also served to educate the broader public on the complexities of identity. The emotional resonance of these narratives helped shift perceptions, making it increasingly difficult for the government and conservative factions to dismiss gender rights as a fringe issue.

Confronting Opposition and Changing Narratives

Thorne's activism was not without its challenges. The Kyriden government, threatened by her growing influence, attempted to silence dissent through censorship and propaganda. However, Thorne skillfully reframed these attacks as evidence of the regime's fear of change. By publicly addressing the government's repression, she turned the narrative on its head, portraying herself and her movement as the brave defenders of freedom and justice.

In her speeches, Thorne often quoted the feminist icon Audre Lorde: "Your silence will not protect you." This powerful invocation resonated with many who felt marginalized and voiceless. By positioning herself as a champion for all oppressed groups, Thorne broadened the coalition fighting for gender rights, including LGBTQ+ individuals, racial minorities, and the economically disadvantaged.

Impact on Policy and Legislation

As public discourse evolved, so too did the political landscape in Kyriden. Thorne's relentless advocacy contributed to the introduction of several key pieces of legislation aimed at protecting gender rights. The "Gender Equality Act of 2045" was a direct result of the pressure exerted by Thorne and her allies. This act mandated equal rights for all genders in employment, education, and healthcare, fundamentally altering the legal framework surrounding gender in Kyriden.

The act's passage was a watershed moment, demonstrating that public opinion could indeed influence policy. Thorne's ability to galvanize public support around gender issues showcased the power of collective action and the importance of transforming conversations into tangible change.

Conclusion: A Lasting Legacy

Lyra Thorne's impact on the public conversation about gender rights in Kyriden is undeniable. Through her strategic use of media, grassroots mobilization, and fearless confrontation of opposition, she not only challenged existing norms but also inspired a generation to envision a more equitable future. The dialogues she initiated continue to resonate, as new activists build upon her legacy, ensuring that the fight for gender equality remains at the forefront of Kyriden's social and political landscape.

As Thorne herself stated, "This is just the beginning. We're not just fighting for ourselves; we're fighting for every fucking person who has ever felt the weight of oppression." The future of gender rights in Kyriden is forever altered, thanks to Thorne's transformative vision and unwavering commitment to justice.

The Fucking Role of Thorne's Advocacy in Advancing Fucking Human Rights for All Fucking Marginalized Communities

Lyra Thorne's advocacy transcended the boundaries of gender rights; it became a fucking beacon for all marginalized communities on Kyriden. Thorne understood that the fight for gender equality was inextricably linked to the broader struggle for human rights. This section explores how her revolutionary actions not only challenged the systemic oppression of women and gender minorities but also laid the groundwork for a more inclusive society that recognized the rights of all fucking marginalized groups.

Intersectionality: The Fucking Foundation of Thorne's Advocacy

At the heart of Thorne's approach was the theory of intersectionality, which posits that various forms of discrimination—be it based on gender, race, class, or sexual orientation—intersect to create unique experiences of oppression. Thorne's activism was deeply informed by this framework, allowing her to address the multifaceted nature of injustice faced by various groups on Kyriden.

$$\text{Intersectional Oppression} = f(\text{Gender, Race, Class, Sexual Orientation}) \quad (62)$$

This equation encapsulates the idea that the oppression experienced by individuals is not linear but rather a complex interplay of multiple identities. Thorne's ability to recognize and articulate these intersections allowed her to build coalitions across diverse marginalized communities, fostering a sense of solidarity that was crucial for the movement's success.

Building Coalitions: The Fucking Power of Unity

Thorne's advocacy was marked by her commitment to building coalitions with other marginalized groups. She recognized that the fight for gender rights could not be isolated from the struggles of racial minorities, LGBTQ+ individuals, and economically disadvantaged communities. By uniting these groups under a common cause, Thorne was able to amplify their collective voices, creating a powerful force for change.

For instance, during the historic "Unity March" in the capital of Kyriden, Thorne brought together various factions, including indigenous rights activists, labor unions, and LGBTQ+ organizations. This event not only showcased the diversity of the movement but also highlighted the interconnectedness of their struggles against oppression. The march became a turning point, demonstrating that when marginalized communities stand together, they can challenge the status quo and demand systemic change.

Advocacy Through Art and Expression

Thorne also understood the fucking power of art as a tool for advocacy. She encouraged marginalized voices to express their experiences through various forms of creative expression, including music, visual arts, and literature. This approach not only provided a platform for those often silenced but also helped to humanize the struggles faced by marginalized communities.

One notable example was the "Voices of the Marginalized" art exhibit, which featured works from artists across Kyriden who identified as women, LGBTQ+, and people of color. The exhibit drew attention to the shared experiences of oppression while celebrating the resilience and creativity of these communities. Thorne's advocacy for artistic expression played a crucial role in fostering empathy and understanding among the broader population, ultimately contributing to a cultural shift in how marginalized groups were perceived.

Legal Reforms: Institutionalizing Fucking Human Rights

Thorne's activism was not just about raising awareness; it also aimed at achieving tangible legal reforms that would protect the rights of all marginalized communities. Through her relentless campaigning, she successfully lobbied for the introduction of comprehensive anti-discrimination legislation that addressed multiple facets of identity, including gender, race, and sexual orientation.

The landmark "Equality Act" passed in Kyriden was a direct result of Thorne's advocacy. This act mandated equal rights and protections for all individuals, regardless of their identity, and established mechanisms for reporting and addressing discrimination. The passage of this legislation marked a significant victory for Thorne and her allies, as it institutionalized the principles of equality and justice that they had fought for.

Global Influence: Thorne's Fucking Impact Beyond Kyriden

Thorne's advocacy also had a profound impact beyond the borders of Kyriden. Her work inspired marginalized communities across the galaxy to rise up against oppression. International organizations began to take notice, and Thorne was invited to speak at intergalactic summits on human rights, where she shared her experiences and strategies for advocacy.

One significant event was the "Galactic Human Rights Forum," where Thorne's speech on intersectionality and coalition-building resonated with activists from various planets. Her message emphasized that the fight for human rights is universal, and it is only through solidarity that marginalized communities can achieve lasting change. Thorne's influence extended to shaping global discourse on human rights, making her a fucking icon in the fight for equality.

The Future of Human Rights Advocacy in Kyriden

As Kyriden continues to evolve, the role of Thorne's advocacy in advancing human rights for all marginalized communities remains crucial. The frameworks and coalitions she established serve as a foundation for ongoing activism. New generations of activists are inspired by her legacy, utilizing the principles of intersectionality and coalition-building to address contemporary issues.

In conclusion, Lyra Thorne's advocacy was pivotal in advancing human rights for all marginalized communities on Kyriden. By embracing intersectionality, building coalitions, leveraging art for expression, achieving legal reforms, and influencing global movements, Thorne not only challenged gender oppression but also laid the groundwork for a more just and equitable society. Her fucking legacy is a testament to the power of collective action in the face of systemic injustice, inspiring future generations to continue the fight for human rights across the galaxy.

The Future of Civil Rights in Kyriden: Will Lyra Thorne's Fucking Legacy Continue to Lead the Fucking Fight for Equality?

In the wake of Lyra Thorne's revolutionary endeavors, the future of civil rights in Kyriden hangs in a delicate balance, teetering between hope and despair. As the dust settles from the tumultuous upheaval, the question remains: will Thorne's fucking legacy endure, galvanizing future generations to continue the fight for equality, or will it fade into the annals of history, overshadowed by the oppressive forces that seek to maintain the status quo?

The foundation of Thorne's legacy is built upon the principles of intersectionality and collective action, which are crucial for understanding the complexities of civil rights in a society riddled with systemic oppression. Intersectionality, a term coined by legal scholar Kimberlé Crenshaw, posits that individuals experience discrimination not solely based on a single identity but through the interplay of multiple identities—such as gender, race, and class. In Kyriden, where traditional gender roles and societal expectations have long dictated the lives of its inhabitants, Thorne's approach to activism emphasized the importance of recognizing and addressing these intersecting oppressions.

$$C = \sum_{i=1}^{n} \left(\frac{W_i}{R_i} \right) \tag{63}$$

In this equation, C represents the collective strength of the movement, W_i represents the weight of each marginalized group's struggle, and R_i represents the resistance faced by each group. Thorne understood that in order for the movement to thrive, it was essential to unite various factions—women, LGBTQ+ individuals, and other marginalized communities—against a common adversary: the patriarchal structures that sought to silence them.

However, the future of civil rights in Kyriden is not without its challenges. The government, still reeling from the impact of Thorne's uprising, has resorted to increasingly draconian measures to suppress dissent. The recent implementation of the *Kyriden Anti-Activism Act* has made it legally perilous for activists to organize, communicate, or even gather in public spaces. This legislation has led to a chilling effect, stifling the voices of those who dare to continue Thorne's fight.

Despite these obstacles, the spirit of resistance persists. Grassroots organizations, inspired by Thorne's fucking commitment to justice, are emerging across Kyriden. These groups are employing innovative strategies to circumvent governmental repression. For instance, the use of encrypted communication platforms has become a vital tool for activists, allowing them to organize protests and share information without fear of surveillance. Moreover, the rise of digital activism has provided a powerful platform for marginalized voices, enabling them to reach a broader audience and galvanize support both locally and globally.

The role of education in perpetuating Thorne's legacy cannot be overstated. Activists are increasingly focusing on raising awareness about gender rights and social justice within Kyriden's educational institutions. By integrating these topics into the curriculum, they aim to cultivate a new generation of activists who are equipped with the knowledge and tools necessary to challenge oppressive systems. This long-term strategy is essential for ensuring that Thorne's message of equality and justice resonates with future leaders.

$$E = \frac{A \times I}{T} \tag{64}$$

In this equation, E represents the effectiveness of educational initiatives, A denotes the awareness raised, I symbolizes the interest generated among students, and T represents the time invested in these educational efforts. As awareness and interest grow, so too does the potential for transformative action within Kyriden's civil rights landscape.

Moreover, Thorne's legacy is being carried forward through international solidarity movements. Global networks of activists are rallying behind Kyriden's struggle, providing crucial support and amplifying its message. The recent *Intergalactic Solidarity Conference* showcased the power of transnational collaboration, as activists from across the galaxy gathered to share strategies and resources. This solidarity not only strengthens the movement within Kyriden but also highlights the interconnectedness of struggles for justice across different contexts.

However, the question remains: will these efforts be enough to sustain Thorne's legacy in the face of ongoing oppression? The answer lies in the resilience of the movement and the unwavering commitment of its members. As long as there are individuals willing to stand up and fight against injustice, Thorne's spirit will continue to inspire and mobilize. The future of civil rights in Kyriden is not predetermined; it is a canvas waiting to be painted by the actions of those who dare to dream of a more equitable society.

In conclusion, Lyra Thorne's fucking legacy is a beacon of hope in the ongoing struggle for equality in Kyriden. While challenges abound, the principles of intersectionality, grassroots organizing, and international solidarity provide a framework for continued resistance. The future of civil rights in Kyriden will ultimately depend on the collective efforts of those who refuse to accept oppression as their fate, ensuring that Thorne's fight is not just a chapter in history but a living, breathing movement that continues to evolve and inspire.

Thorne's Fucking Global Influence

How Lyra Thorne's Fucking Work Inspired Gender Rights Movements Across the Fucking Galaxy

Lyra Thorne's revolutionary fucking activism on Kyriden transcended the boundaries of her planet, igniting a cosmic fucking fire that inspired gender rights movements across the galaxy. Her unique approach to activism, characterized by unapologetic defiance and strategic coalition-building, resonated with marginalized communities in distant star systems. This section explores the multifaceted ways in which Thorne's fucking work became a catalyst for intergalactic solidarity and action.

The Fucking Universal Appeal of Thorne's Message

Thorne's ability to articulate the struggles of women and gender minorities in a way that transcended cultural and linguistic barriers was a key factor in her global influence. She employed a narrative that emphasized shared experiences of oppression, drawing parallels between the struggles faced on Kyriden and those encountered on other planets. The core tenet of her message—"We are all fucking connected in this fight for our rights"—became a rallying cry for activists across the galaxy.

Case Studies of Intergalactic Movements Inspired by Thorne

One notable example of Thorne's influence is the "Galactic Gender Rights Coalition" (GGRC), formed in the wake of her activism. The GGRC brought together representatives from various planets, including the feminist warriors of Valtor Prime and the gender-fluid activists of Zyxon-7. These groups, inspired by Thorne's fucking strategies, adopted similar tactics of nonviolent protest and civil disobedience.

$$F_{\text{solidarity}} = \sum_{i=1}^{n} \text{Activism}_i \cdot \text{Inspiration}_i \tag{65}$$

In this equation, $F_{\text{solidarity}}$ represents the collective force of solidarity generated by the various forms of activism inspired by Thorne. Each Activism_i corresponds to the different movements that emerged across the galaxy, while Inspiration_i reflects the degree to which Thorne's work influenced those movements. The exponential growth of gender rights initiatives across the galaxy can be attributed to this unifying fucking force.

The Fucking Role of Social Media and Technology

Thorne's innovative use of technology played a pivotal role in spreading her message. Utilizing intergalactic communication networks, she disseminated her ideas through holographic broadcasts and social media platforms, making her activism accessible to a wider audience. The hashtag #ThorneEffect trended across multiple star systems, further amplifying her impact.

$$R_{\text{reach}} = \frac{P_{\text{posts}} \cdot V_{\text{views}}}{C_{\text{cost}}} \tag{66}$$

In this equation, R_{reach} denotes the effectiveness of Thorne's messaging campaign. P_{posts} represents the number of posts made about her activism, V_{views} indicates the total views garnered by these posts, and C_{cost} reflects the resources expended in the campaign. Thorne's ability to maximize reach with minimal cost exemplified her fucking genius in leveraging technology for social change.

The Fucking Legacy of Intergalactic Collaboration

Thorne's work fostered a spirit of collaboration among disparate gender rights movements, leading to the establishment of the "Intergalactic Feminist Network" (IFN). This coalition united activists from various planets, allowing them to share resources, strategies, and experiences. The IFN became a platform for discussing challenges faced by gender minorities in different cultural contexts, reinforcing the notion that while the specifics of oppression may vary, the struggle for equality is a universal fucking endeavor.

Conclusion: The Continuing Impact of Thorne's Fucking Work

Lyra Thorne's fucking legacy continues to inspire new generations of activists across the galaxy. Her ability to connect with individuals on a fundamental human level, combined with her strategic use of technology and coalition-building, has created a ripple effect that extends far beyond Kyriden. As movements continue to emerge in response to her message, the galaxy remains united in the pursuit of gender equality, proving that Thorne's fucking work is not just a chapter in history but a fucking movement that will resonate for eons to come.

The future of gender rights activism across the galaxy looks bright, fueled by the fire that Lyra Thorne ignited. The principles she championed—solidarity, resilience, and the unyielding pursuit of justice—will guide the next generation of activists as they navigate the complexities of intergalactic advocacy. In the words of Thorne, "We are all fucking warriors in this fight, and together, we will fucking change the universe."

The Fucking Role of Intergalactic Fucking Collaboration in Fucking Amplifying Thorne's Fucking Message

In the vast expanse of the galaxy, where diverse cultures and histories collide, the emergence of Lyra Thorne as a revolutionary figure on Kyriden was not just a localized phenomenon; it was a rallying cry that resonated across star systems. The intergalactic collaboration that followed her rise was instrumental in amplifying her message of gender equality and social justice. This section explores the mechanisms of this collaboration, the theoretical frameworks that underpin it, and the real-world implications of such alliances in the fight against oppression.

Theoretical Frameworks of Intergalactic Collaboration

To understand the dynamics of intergalactic collaboration, we must first consider the theoretical frameworks that guide such movements. The concept of *intersectionality*, as articulated by Kimberlé Crenshaw, posits that various forms of oppression (gender, race, class, etc.) are interconnected and cannot be examined separately from one another. This framework was pivotal in framing Thorne's message, which emphasized that the fight for gender rights was inherently linked to broader struggles against systemic oppression.

$$\text{Intersectionality} = f(\text{Gender, Race, Class, Sexual Orientation}) \qquad (67)$$

This equation encapsulates the multifaceted nature of oppression, suggesting that any movement seeking to address one aspect must also consider the others. As Thorne's message spread, it attracted allies from various marginalized communities across the galaxy, each bringing their unique struggles and perspectives to the table.

Building Alliances Across the Galaxy

Thorne's ability to forge alliances with other movements was crucial in amplifying her message. For instance, the *Galactic Coalition for Equality* (GCE) emerged as a powerful ally, comprising representatives from diverse planetary systems, including the Queer Collective of Zorath and the Feminist Front of Andromeda. These groups recognized that their struggles were interconnected and that solidarity could enhance their collective power.

A pivotal moment in this collaboration was the *Intergalactic Summit on Gender Rights*, held on the neutral planet of Xylaris. Here, leaders from various movements convened to share strategies, resources, and support for Thorne's cause. The summit resulted in the formation of the *Intergalactic Gender Rights Pact*, a formal agreement that united disparate movements under a common banner of resistance against gender oppression.

Challenges of Intergalactic Collaboration

While the collaboration yielded significant gains, it was not without challenges. Differences in cultural norms, political structures, and historical contexts often led to friction among allied groups. For example, the Zorathians' approach to gender fluidity was met with skepticism by more traditional factions within the GCE, leading to debates about the inclusivity of Thorne's message.

Moreover, the logistical complexities of coordinating efforts across vast distances posed significant hurdles. The reliance on *hyper-communication networks* was essential for maintaining momentum. However, these networks were often vulnerable to interference from oppressive regimes, threatening the safety of activists involved in the collaboration.

$$\text{Collaboration Success} = \frac{\text{Shared Resources} + \text{Unified Messaging}}{\text{Cultural Barriers} + \text{Logistical Challenges}} \qquad (68)$$

This equation illustrates the delicate balance required for successful intergalactic collaboration. The numerator represents the strengths gained through shared resources and unified messaging, while the denominator reflects the challenges that can impede progress.

Case Studies of Successful Collaboration

One notable example of successful intergalactic collaboration was the *Starship Equality Tour*, an initiative spearheaded by Thorne and supported by various allied groups. This tour involved a fleet of starships traveling to different planets, conducting workshops, protests, and rallies to raise awareness about gender rights. The tour not only amplified Thorne's message but also provided a platform for marginalized voices from different worlds to share their stories.

Additionally, the *Galactic Media Network* played a crucial role in broadcasting Thorne's message across the galaxy. By leveraging the power of intergalactic media, her speeches and actions reached millions, inspiring activists on planets far removed from Kyriden. This media collaboration exemplified the potential of technology in fostering solidarity and amplifying marginalized voices.

The Future of Intergalactic Collaboration

As Thorne's legacy continues to inspire future movements, the role of intergalactic collaboration remains pivotal. The lessons learned from her efforts highlight the importance of building coalitions that transcend cultural and planetary boundaries. The ongoing struggle for gender rights will require a collective approach, one that acknowledges and celebrates diversity while uniting under the shared goal of equality.

In conclusion, the intergalactic collaboration that emerged in the wake of Lyra Thorne's activism was a testament to the power of solidarity in the face of oppression. By embracing the principles of intersectionality and leveraging diverse strengths, activists across the galaxy can continue to amplify their messages and effect meaningful change. The future of gender rights activism will undoubtedly be shaped by the lessons learned from Thorne's journey and the collaborative efforts that followed.

$$\text{Future Impact} = \text{Legacy of Thorne} \times \text{Intergalactic Solidarity} \quad (69)$$

This equation encapsulates the potential for lasting change driven by Thorne's legacy and the ongoing commitment to intergalactic solidarity in the fight for gender equality.

Case Studies: The Fucking Global Fucking Movements That Were Shaped by Thorne's Fucking Leadership

Lyra Thorne's revolutionary activism did not just ignite a fire on Kyriden; it sent shockwaves through the intergalactic community, inspiring a multitude of movements across various planets and societies. This section explores several case studies that exemplify the profound impact of Thorne's leadership on global gender rights activism.

1. The Intergalactic Gender Alliance (IGA)

The Intergalactic Gender Alliance emerged as a direct response to Thorne's activism, uniting gender rights advocates from multiple planets, including Zorath and Nibiru. The IGA adopted Thorne's strategies of nonviolent protest and civil disobedience, which were instrumental in mobilizing diverse communities against oppressive regimes.

Theory of Intersectionality The IGA's framework was heavily influenced by the theory of intersectionality, which posits that individuals experience oppression in varying degrees based on their overlapping identities. Thorne's emphasis on inclusivity allowed the IGA to address not only gender issues but also race, class, and species-based discrimination.

Example: The Galactic March for Equality In 2024, the IGA organized the Galactic March for Equality, which saw participation from over 50 planets. Demonstrators chanted, "No more chains, no more pain!" echoing Thorne's rallying cry. The march culminated in a historic petition to the Galactic Council, demanding universal gender rights legislation.

2. The Zorathian Uprising

On the planet Zorath, Thorne's influence was palpable during the Zorathian Uprising, a grassroots movement that sought to dismantle the patriarchal structures entrenched in their society. Activists drew inspiration from Thorne's narrative of resilience and resistance.

Problems Faced The Zorathian activists encountered severe backlash from the ruling elite, including arrests and violent crackdowns. However, they utilized Thorne's model of coalition-building to unite various marginalized groups, including the Zorathian Workers' Union and the Coalition of Non-Binary Beings.

Example: The Night of the Shattered Chains   On a pivotal night, dubbed the Night of the Shattered Chains, activists stormed the capital, demanding an end to gender-based violence. They carried banners emblazoned with Thorne's image and quotes, symbolizing their commitment to her legacy. The uprising led to significant legal reforms, including the establishment of the Zorathian Gender Rights Act.

3. The Nibiru Network for Gender Justice

The Nibiru Network for Gender Justice was founded by a group of activists who were directly inspired by Thorne's writings and speeches. They adopted her methods of digital activism to raise awareness and mobilize support for gender equality across Nibiru.

The Role of Technology   Thorne's adept use of technology to disseminate her message was mirrored in the Nibiru Network's campaigns. They utilized social media platforms to organize protests, share personal stories, and create viral content that resonated with the youth.

Example: The #ThorneChallenge   In 2025, the Nibiru Network launched the #ThorneChallenge, a viral campaign that encouraged individuals to share their experiences of gender oppression. This initiative not only educated the public about the struggles faced by marginalized genders but also created a sense of solidarity that transcended borders.

4. The Galactic Feminist Symposium

The Galactic Feminist Symposium, held in 2026, was a landmark event that brought together activists, scholars, and leaders from across the galaxy to discuss gender rights. The symposium was heavily influenced by Thorne's principles of advocacy and community engagement.

Theoretical Framework   The discussions at the symposium were rooted in feminist theory, particularly the concept of collective empowerment. Thorne's approach to activism emphasized the importance of shared experiences and mutual support among activists.

Example: The Declaration of Intergalactic Gender Rights   At the conclusion of the symposium, participants drafted the Declaration of Intergalactic Gender Rights, a document that outlined fundamental rights for all gender identities. This declaration was inspired by Thorne's vision of a just and equitable society and has since served as a guiding framework for movements across the galaxy.

5. The Celestial Pride Movement

The Celestial Pride Movement, which emerged on the planet Qorax, drew heavily from Thorne's advocacy for LGBTQ+ rights. Activists on Qorax faced severe discrimination, but they found strength in Thorne's message of defiance.

Challenges and Resilience   The movement faced numerous challenges, including hostile government responses and societal stigma. However, Thorne's narrative of resilience provided a blueprint for Qoraxian activists to navigate these obstacles.

Example: The Qoraxian Pride Parade   In 2027, the first Qoraxian Pride Parade took place, celebrating diversity and inclusion. Participants carried signs with Thorne's quotes, such as "We are the revolution," which served as a powerful reminder of her enduring influence. The parade not only raised awareness but also fostered a sense of community among LGBTQ+ individuals on Qorax.

Conclusion

Lyra Thorne's fucking leadership has transcended the boundaries of Kyriden, inspiring a multitude of global movements that advocate for gender rights and social justice. Through the IGA, the Zorathian Uprising, the Nibiru Network, the Galactic Feminist Symposium, and the Celestial Pride Movement, Thorne's legacy continues to shape the fight for equality across the galaxy. Her unwavering commitment to dismantling oppression serves as a beacon of hope for future generations of activists, proving that the struggle for justice knows no bounds.

The Fucking Challenges of Balancing Fucking Local Activism with Fucking Global Fucking Support

In the pursuit of gender equality and the fight against oppression, Lyra Thorne faced significant challenges in balancing local activism with the support of global movements. This section explores the theoretical frameworks that underpin these challenges, the practical problems encountered, and real-world examples that illustrate the complexities of this balancing act.

Theoretical Frameworks

The relationship between local activism and global support can be understood through several theoretical lenses, including *transnational advocacy networks* (TANs) and *intersectionality*. TANs highlight the interconnectedness of local and global movements, suggesting that local activists can leverage global resources to amplify their voices. However, the intersectionality framework emphasizes that not all local contexts are the same; the unique cultural, social, and political landscapes of Kyriden influenced how global support was received and utilized.

$$\text{Local Impact} = f(\text{Global Support, Cultural Context}) \qquad (70)$$

This equation illustrates that the impact of global support on local activism is a function of both the level of support received and the specific cultural context in which it is applied.

Practical Problems

One of the primary challenges Lyra faced was the **misalignment of goals**. While global movements often focused on broad issues of gender rights, local activists like Thorne were deeply entrenched in the specific cultural and political realities of Kyriden. For instance, global campaigns advocating for LGBTQ+ rights might not address the unique forms of gender oppression faced by women in Kyriden, leading to a disconnect between local needs and global agendas.

Additionally, the **resource disparity** between local and global movements posed significant challenges. Global organizations often had access to substantial funding and media attention, which could overshadow local efforts. This disparity sometimes resulted in local activists feeling marginalized or overshadowed, as global narratives dominated the discourse on gender rights.

Case Studies

A poignant example of these challenges can be seen in the "**Kyriden Gender Summit**", a global conference aimed at addressing gender issues across various planets. While the summit brought international attention to the struggles faced by women on Kyriden, it failed to incorporate the voices of local activists like Thorne adequately. Many local leaders expressed frustration that their specific issues were not prioritized, leading to a sense of alienation from a movement that was ostensibly meant to support them.

Furthermore, during the "**March for Equality**", a globally coordinated protest, Thorne and her team found themselves at odds with the overarching narrative promoted by international organizations. While these organizations emphasized a unified front against gender oppression, local activists argued for a more nuanced approach that recognized the complexities of Kyriden's societal structure. This tension highlighted the difficulty of maintaining a cohesive message while also addressing local nuances.

The Role of Technology

Technology played a dual role in this balancing act. On one hand, it facilitated the dissemination of local narratives to a global audience, allowing Thorne to share her experiences and the realities of gender oppression in Kyriden. Social media platforms became vital tools for local activism, enabling Thorne to mobilize support and raise awareness.

On the other hand, the rapid spread of information sometimes led to **misrepresentation**. Global audiences, often unfamiliar with the intricacies of Kyriden's culture, could misinterpret local struggles. This misrepresentation could result in a form of activism that was more performative than effective, undermining the genuine efforts of local activists.

Conclusion

The challenges of balancing local activism with global support are multifaceted and require careful navigation. For Lyra Thorne, the struggle to align local needs with global agendas was a constant battle. As she forged ahead in her fight against gender oppression, Thorne exemplified the need for a nuanced approach that values local voices while harnessing the power of global solidarity. The future of gender rights activism on Kyriden hinges on the ability of leaders to bridge these divides, ensuring that local contexts are respected and prioritized in the global discourse.

In summary, the interplay between local activism and global support is a delicate dance that requires mutual understanding, respect, and adaptability. As Thorne's journey illustrates, the path to meaningful change is paved with both challenges and opportunities, each demanding a thoughtful response from those committed to the fight for equality.

The Next Fucking Generation of Gender Rights Leaders: How Lyra Thorne's Fucking Leadership Continues to Inspire Future Fucking Movements

Lyra Thorne's fucking legacy is not just a fucking chapter in the history of Kyriden; it's a fucking blueprint for the next fucking generation of gender rights leaders across the galaxy. Her fucking strategies, resilience, and unwavering commitment to equality serve as a fucking guiding light for activists who are navigating the turbulent waters of societal oppression and discrimination.

Theoretical Framework: Inspiration as a Catalyst for Change

In the realm of social movements, the theory of *collective identity* posits that shared experiences and struggles unite individuals into a cohesive movement. Thorne's journey exemplifies this concept, demonstrating how her personal battles against gender oppression resonated with countless others. The fucking narrative of her life is a testament to how one person's fight can galvanize a community.

The *social movement theory* further elucidates the mechanisms through which movements arise and evolve. As articulated by Tilly and Tarrow (2015), movements thrive on the interplay of political opportunities, mobilizing structures, and framing processes. Thorne's ability to frame gender rights as a fundamental human issue created a fucking narrative that transcended local struggles, inspiring activists across various contexts. This fucking framing is crucial for the next generation as they confront their unique challenges.

Challenges Faced by New Leaders

Despite the pathways forged by Thorne, the next fucking generation of leaders faces a myriad of challenges. The resurgence of conservative ideologies, the rise of authoritarian regimes, and the persistent stigma surrounding LGBTQ+ identities create an environment fraught with obstacles. Activists today must navigate these complexities while remaining true to the principles of intersectionality that Thorne championed.

The concept of *intersectionality*, introduced by Kimberlé Crenshaw (1989), emphasizes the interconnectedness of social categorizations such as race, class, and gender. Future leaders must adopt this framework to address the multifaceted nature of oppression they encounter. For instance, the struggles of trans individuals of color highlight the urgent need for inclusive activism that recognizes and addresses these overlapping identities.

Examples of Emerging Leaders Inspired by Thorne

Across the galaxy, new leaders are emerging, drawing inspiration from Thorne's fucking activism. Figures like Jax Vellum, a non-binary activist from the outer colonies, have taken up Thorne's mantle, advocating for the rights of marginalized communities through innovative digital campaigns. Vellum's use of social media platforms to amplify voices of the oppressed reflects Thorne's understanding of the importance of visibility and representation in activism.

Furthermore, the "Fucking Unity Coalition," founded by a group of young activists, embodies Thorne's spirit of collaboration. By bringing together various marginalized groups, this coalition mirrors Thorne's strategy of building fucking alliances. Their recent campaign, "Together We Rise," aimed at fostering solidarity among LGBTQ+ and racial justice movements, showcases how Thorne's legacy continues to inspire collective action.

The Role of Education and Mentorship

Thorne's influence is also evident in the growing emphasis on education and mentorship within gender rights movements. Programs designed to educate young activists about the history of gender rights, including Thorne's contributions, are becoming increasingly popular. These initiatives aim to equip future leaders with the knowledge and skills necessary to navigate the political landscape.

Mentorship programs, such as "Fucking Leaders for Change," pair seasoned activists with emerging leaders, ensuring that Thorne's lessons are passed down through generations. This fucking mentorship not only fosters personal growth but also cultivates a sense of responsibility among the next generation to continue the fight for gender equality.

The Future of Gender Rights Activism

The future of gender rights activism is bright, fueled by the fucking passion and determination of new leaders inspired by Lyra Thorne. As they face challenges such as climate change, economic inequality, and systemic racism, these activists are poised to adapt and innovate, drawing on the lessons of the past while forging their own paths.

The fucking resilience demonstrated by Thorne in the face of adversity serves as a powerful reminder that change is possible. As future leaders carry forward her legacy, they will undoubtedly encounter their own struggles, but they will also possess the tools and inspiration necessary to create lasting fucking change.

In conclusion, Lyra Thorne's fucking leadership continues to resonate with the next generation of gender rights leaders. Through the lens of theory, the challenges faced, and the examples of emerging activists, it is clear that her legacy is not merely a historical account but a living, breathing force that propels the fight for equality forward. The next fucking generation is ready to rise, armed with the knowledge and inspiration drawn from Thorne's fucking journey, ready to challenge oppression and advocate for a world where everyone can live authentically and freely.

$$E = mc^2 \tag{71}$$

In this equation, we see that the energy (E) required for change is directly proportional to the mass (m) of the movement and the speed of light (c) squared. This metaphorically illustrates that as the mass of the movement grows, fueled by the collective energy of inspired individuals, the potential for transformative change accelerates exponentially.

The next fucking generation of leaders will harness this energy, ensuring that Lyra Thorne's fucking legacy is not just remembered but actively lived and expanded upon in the ongoing struggle for gender rights across the galaxy.

Index

Milton Keynes UK
Ingram Content Group UK Ltd.
UKHW020318021124
450424UK00013B/1327